ASPATORE
C-Level Business Intelligence™

Praise for Books, Business Intelligence Publications & Services

"A valuable probe into the thought, perspectives, and techniques of accomplished professionals...the authors place their endeavors in a context rarely gleaned from text books or treatises." - Charles Birenbaum, Labor Chair, Thelen Reid & Priest

"A rare peek behind the curtains and into the minds of the industry's best." - Brandon Baum, Partner, Cooley Godward

"Tremendous insights...a must read..." - James Quinn, Litigation Chair, Weil, Gotshal & Manges

"Unlike any other business book..." - Bruce Keller, IP Litigation Chair, Debevoise & Plimpton

"Intensely personal, practical advice from seasoned dealmakers." - Mary Ann Jorgenson, Coordinator of Business Practice Area, Squire, Sanders & Dempsey

"An informative insider's perspective..." - Gary Klotz, Labor Chair, Butzel Long

"A must read..." - Raymond Wheeler, Labor Chair, Morrison & Foerster

"Great practical advise and thoughtful insights." - Mark Gruhin, Partner, Schmeltzer, Aptaker & Shepard, P.C.

"Useful and understandable insight..." - Stuart Lubitz, Partner, Hogan & Hartson, Co-Head of Litigation, Simpson Thacher & Bartlett

ASPATORE
C-Level Business Intelligence™

Publisher of Books, Business Intelligence Publications & Services

www.Aspatore.com

Aspatore is the world's largest and most exclusive publisher of C-Level executives (CEO, CFO, CTO, CMO, Partner) from the world's most respected companies. Aspatore annually publishes C-Level executives from over half the Global 500, top 250 professional services firms, law firms (MPs/Chairs), and other leading companies of all sizes in books, briefs, reports, articles and other publications. By focusing on publishing only C-Level executives, Aspatore provides professionals of all levels with proven business intelligence from industry insiders, rather than relying on the knowledge of unknown authors and analysts. Aspatore publishes an innovative line of business intelligence resources including Inside the Minds, Bigwig Briefs, ExecRecs, Business Travel Bible, Brainstormers, The C-Level Test, and Aspatore Business Reviews, in addition to other best selling business books, briefs and essays. Aspatore also provides an array of business services including The C-Level Library, PIA Reports, ExecEnablers, and The C-Level Review, as well as outsourced business library and researching capabilities. Aspatore focuses on traditional print publishing and providing business intelligence services, while our portfolio companies, Corporate Publishing Group (B2B writing & editing) and Aspatore Stores and Seminars focus on developing areas within the business and publishing worlds.

BIGWIG BRIEFS TEST PREP:
THE LSAT EXAM

Real World Intelligence, Strategies & Experience From
Industry Experts to Prepare You for Everything the
Classroom and Textbooks Won't Teach You

ASPATORE
C-Level Business Intelligence™

Published by Aspatore Books, Inc.
For information on bulk orders, sponsorship opportunities or any other questions please email store@aspatore.com. For corrections, company/title up1 dates, comments or any other inquiries please email info@aspatore.com.

First Printing, 2002
10 9 8 7 6 5 4 3 2 1

ISBN 1-58762-211-4

Edited By Laurie Mingolelli

Cover design by Rachel Kashon, Kara Yates, Ian Mazie

Material in this book is for educational purposes only. This book is sold with the understanding that neither any of the interviewees or the publisher is engaged in rendering legal, accounting, investment, or any other professional service.

This book is printed on acid free paper.

Special thanks also to: Ted Juliano, Tracy Carbone, and Rinad Beidas

The views expressed by the individuals in this book do not necessarily reflect the views shared by the companies they are employed by (or the companies mentioned in this book). The companies referenced may not be the same company that the individual works for since the publishing of this book.

The views expressed by the endorsements on the cover and in this book are from the book the original content appeared in and do not necessarily reflect the views shared by the companies they are employed by.

BIGWIG BRIEFS TEST PREP:
THE LSAT EXAM

CONTENTS

BIGWIG BRIEFS TEST PREP:
THE LSAT EXAM

How To Use This Book

Bigwig Briefs Test Prep: The LSAT Exam features selections of condensed business intelligence from top industry insiders and is the best way for emerging legal professionals to learn to think, analyze, and respond to situations they will confront in the workplace. The purpose of this book is not to devise the quickest way to answer a LSAT logic question. Our strategy is geared towards the long-term, not the multiple choice quick-fix. We don't tell you how to fill in the dots and mark the grids; that you can find in a classroom or other books. Rather, we try to guide you towards assuming the mindset of the industry's most elite and successful professionals. If you learn to think like a successful lawyer and approach decision-making firmly rooted in this mindset, you greatly increase your chances of having success on your LSAT Exam, especially in answering the difficult questions that are impossible to study for. The authors in this book know what it takes to succeed; now you'll know their secrets, too. Use this information to get an edge and enable yourself to think like a lawyer when taking the LSAT Exam.

Rob Johnson, Sonnenschein Nath & Rosenthal, Chair, Litigation and Business Regulation Practice Group

A Lawyer's Dual Personality: Advocate and Counselor

After over almost 30 years of litigating, I have learned that taking my client's cause and making it my own is of utmost importance in arriving at a successful result. It is essential that a trial lawyer identify with his or her own client and believe in the case. Lawyers that are able to do that can be forceful advocates.

But an effective litigator has to be more than just an advocate; he or she must be the client's counselor as well. This dual role, being the client's champion on the one hand, but on the other hand having to explain to the client the problems and weaknesses in the case and advising the client as to the possibility of settlement, can create a tension that is sometimes uncomfortable for the lawyer. This is because lawyers know that their clients want them to believe in their cause and to support it 100 percent. But good lawyers also understand that it is imperative for them to provide their client with a realistic evaluation of their client's case.

Counseling the client has its rewards for the lawyer as well as the client. The relationship between lawyer and client is truly unique—one in which confidences are given and kept, and sober advice bestowed and taken. The result can be the creation of a bond between the lawyer and client that is valued by both, and can last long after the case is over.

Charles E. Koob, Simpson Thacher & Bartlett, Co-Head of Litigation Department

A Successful Approach to Litigation

My approach to trials is to approach them as theater, and I do not mean that in any negative or demeaning sense. The role of a trial lawyer is to produce a play that informs, entertains, and persuades the finder of fact. By the time a case gets to trial, it is not about the law anymore; it is about the facts and the credibility of witnesses. Cases are won or lost because juries believe one side or the other, not because the law favors one side or the other.

A play has to be choreographed. It must ultimately be designed to persuade someone, whether a judge or jury. Your job as a trial lawyer is to put on an entertaining, convincing, and understandable play. You have to know precisely what you want to achieve with each witness, what piece of the puzzle his testimony represents. When a lawyer is putting on his direct case, all he really is doing is putting witnesses on as actors in his play. They have lines to speak and while you have helped them to be effective in presenting their story, it is, after all, their story. When the other side's witnesses take the stand, the lawyer becomes an actor in the play. Cross-examination should be designed to get the other side's witness to agree with your version of the facts. In effect, you tell the witness what the facts are and get them to agree with you. To be effective at cross-examination, you can never ask a question to which you do not know the answer, and you had better have a document or deposition testimony where the witness has previously given you the answer you want.

Long before the actual trial, a lawyer needs to come up with a theme, a plot for a compelling story. You cannot go into a trial without a very simple, deliverable, straightforward theme about what it is you are going to say to that judge or jury. That theme has to be simple and has to be communicated over and over again. Remember that no matter how long you have been working on your case, you are only going to have the jury for a few days or few weeks. Everything you say to that jury has to be directly related to a story that is easy to tell and easy to grasp. It should be clear to every juror what is important about every witness' testimony, about every document. You never want a witness to leave the stand with a juror wondering what his testimony was all about. The problem I've seen with a lot of trials is that the theme gets lost because there isn't a focus on exactly what the theme is. You have just conducted five years of discovery, and you have all these documents and all these witnesses, and somehow you think you have to get it all into evidence because you've spent so much time immersed in it. Lawyers need to figure out what their theme is and how they are going to try to communicate to the jury in a way that keeps things as simple as possible. It is all about distilling, condensing and eliminating the non-essential.

I have a couple of rules I try to follow when I try cases. One is that I never want to introduce into evidence more documents than I absolutely have to; 100 documents seems like a good goal to have in mind. No matter how many documents have been produced, never introduce more than a few. People simply can't absorb in the course of a trial what it took you years to absorb in preparation. If you want them to focus on something, then you have to limit what it is you show them.

The second rule has to do with direct examination. Get the witness on and off the stand in less than two hours. People do not have the patience to sit and listen to a lawyer and witness drone on and on about the facts. Obviously there are exceptions to this. There are occasions and times when people will have to be on the witness stand longer; but, by and large, if you look at the way most people testify in a courtroom, the import of what they say is delivered in an hour or two.

On cross-examination, it is even more important to get on and get off. I always tell juries that what they really ought to pay attention to during the course of a trial is the cross-examination, because that is when the lawyers are testing the truth of what the other party's witnesses are saying. Your own witness, presumably, will be telling a rehearsed story that you and they have prepared. Juries and judges know direct testimony is prepared testimony. Cross-examination provides an opportunity to test the credibility of your opponent's witnesses and their versions of the facts. In fact, you should probably spend more time preparing your witnesses for cross-examination than you do for direct examination. If your witnesses do well on cross, then the value of their testimony on direct is immeasurably enhanced. Cases by and large are won and lost on cross-examination, not direct examination. My goal on cross-examination, again, is to keep it short. I try to get on and off the stage in an hour. Juries just don't pay attention beyond that.

There is a corollary to the principle: know when to stop. Trial lawyers have a tendency to try to do too much, to ask just one more question. Sometimes it backfires. If you have gotten what you need from a witness, don't try to do more. End on a high note, don't drone on until the jury has lost the impact of your presentation.

I recall a criminal price-fixing trial I had in Milwaukee a few years ago. This was a classic conspiracy case in which I represented the corporate defendant. The government's case consisted of a dozen witnesses. I was convinced that my co-counsel and I had done an effective job of cross-examining those witnesses. I thought we had made our case with them. I had prepared another dozen or so witnesses whom I intended to call as part of my defense, each of whom I had worked with and prepared extensively. I thought our case was pretty compelling; but you never know what will happen on cross-examination. My co-counsel and I agreed we would rest after the government's case. My decision was based on my belief that the government's case had several holes that I did not want to risk having filled with my own witnesses. My client was much less convinced than I was and began a very long evening by insisting that we put on our own case. Twelve hours later, the client reluctantly agreed. We rested without putting on a case. The jury deliberated for less than an hour and came back with a defendants' verdict: not guilty. After the trial, one juror told me that we had convinced the jury following cross-examination of the government's chief witness.

Remember too that consumers today are visual and so are jurors. Just look at the difference between the *Wall Street Journal* and *USA Today*. Jurors approach trials in living color. An endless stream of words is lost on them. Information is also absorbed in short bursts and is more easily absorbed if it is visually accessible. Graphic evidence, if not overdone, can be a tremendous aid in telling your story.

I should also say at least a few words about experts. Most of the cases in which I am involved are complex. Most require experts. This is particularly true in antitrust cases, which, in today's legal climate, focus on economics and economic theory. Involve your expert early whether you are a plaintiff or a defendant. If you are a plaintiff, have your expert help draft your complaint. If you don't, you may have to live with a pleading that describes a theory your expert cannot support. Secondly, make sure your expert sees *all* of the evidence. The most effective cross-examination of experts occurs when they have not taken the time to immerse themselves in the facts. This is particularly true with some academic experts who never seem to have enough time to immerse themselves in the facts. Third, make sure your expert understands that at trial he is there to explain, not to impress jurors with his résumé. Choosing experts who can and do teach, particularly at the undergraduate level, can make your task much easier.

The Most Important Things to Know as a Litigator

The very best litigators I have ever seen and the ones I admire the most are the ones who are good storytellers. The best advice I ever received was that effective trial work depends on developing a good theme. The theme guides your entire effort. Everything has to revolve around a very simple theme that you are prepared to make the central core to your case. If you do that, your case has direction and focus, and if you don't, it has no focus and you will lose your audience. That's hard to do at the beginning. At the beginning, litigation requires a tremendous amount of thought. It's like building a house. You don't build a house without architectural plans, and the better the plans, the less trouble you have in building the house. You get your architect to come in and draw plans for you, and you make changes to the house at the architectural stage, not when the roof is on. Litigation and particularly trial work are no different. Planning and preparation in litigation for every step you take is critical. You have to have a plan and follow it; and the better you plan, the more prepared you are, the better the result. Trial work is not something you can do by the seat of your pants.

I also want to return to a theme I mentioned earlier. Lawyers, at their best, are problem solvers. In a real sense, lawyers are social plumbers. They fix the jams in society's pipes. The problem with many lawyers is that when clients come to them, they immediately focus on the problem as a legal issue. It may or may not be; but even if it is, the legal solution has to be viewed in context. Clients' problems are seldom solved by having lawyers run to the law books or throw search words into a computer and having computers spit out cases. When I give what I consider to be a fairly complex issue to a young associate, the first thing I have him do is leave the building for an hour, take a walk around the block, take a run around Central Park, and think about the problem before looking for a solution. If you don't understand the problem and the context in which it arose, then you are never going to understand the solution. Lawyers, at their best, are problem solvers, and problem solvers have to think about solutions in the context of the complicated social network in which the problem arose.

Think before you act. Develop a clear, concise, simple theme. Believe in it and stick with it. Be yourself. To me, those are the most important rules.

John Strauch, Jones, Day, Reavis & Pogue, Firmwide Chairman of the Litigation Department

The Secrets of Successful Litigation Attorneys

First and foremost, you must have the quality of empathy with other people, the capacity to identify with, connect with, understand, impress, and gain the trust of other people. Ultimately, that puts you in a position to be able to persuade another person, a judge, or a jury, of the correctness and justness of your position. With a client or a witness, your empathy engenders in them a degree of trust in you that permits them to follow your advice and to become prepared enough to deal with the problem as they need to, avoiding things that get in the way of appropriate communication. With an adverse witness you are cross-examining, it allows you to step into his or her shoes, feel the other's perspective, and do a better job of cross-examination, seeing avenues to explore you might otherwise miss.

A second requirement is a high degree of intelligence, with an ability to see fine distinctions; to analyze things very carefully and sharply and finely; to determine the existence or absence of important contradictions; and to prioritize from the best, most relevant arguments to those less so for purposes of deciding how you're going to spend your time and your credibility.

One of the great enemies of winning is the fear of losing. Another is refusing to let go of any argument you can make or any facts you can present so that if you do lose, you're not criticized for not throwing everything you could have at the problem. That's not ever a good approach. You have to prioritize; you have to let go of some things; you have to make certain you're not flooding your best arguments and your best facts with a sea of much less important, less persuasive arguments and facts.

Alongside intelligence, you need quickness of wit and nimbleness of mind. There are lots of intelligent people who are probably a lot smarter than I and other trial lawyers are, who couldn't begin to try a case or cross-examine a witness. They may be extremely intelligent or extremely adept at going through all the analysis that might be a part of this process if they have the time, and if they can do it under controlled circumstances of peace and quiet. That's very different from having to make split-second decisions in a courtroom, when you're cross-examining a witness or responding to a judge's questions, or even delivering a closing argument to a jury, which is prepared to some extent, but you have to have some flexibility in mind. So on top of the intelligence, you also have to have this quickness of mind and nimbleness of wit that allows you to very quickly adjust your thinking and take different courses of action and make split-second decisions under fire in a very public way and in very tense situations—all of which may be complicated by a judge who's hostile to you or a circumstance that has surprised you.

Another quality, especially with respect to the kind of litigation my firm specializes in—very complex, often multijurisdictional, high-stakes, heavily documentary litigation—is the capacity to manage people and information systems and establish efficient systems that give a client the highest possible effectiveness for the dollar. When I started practicing 36 years ago, that wasn't so important. You didn't have mammoth, nationwide class-actions, or multijurisdictional litigation being multidistricted in a single court for purposes of discovery, and an untold number of cases being brought together like that or pending in many separate courts. Now you do. To be a good litigator, you also need to have that kind of operations-officer capability.

Different, but along the same lines, is the need for a strategic sense, as well as a tactical sense, and the larger the case, the more critical this quality is. You need to be able to see the big picture, engage in broad planning, and know the general theme and direction your case will take. That's in addition to having a fine tactical sense, which is more related to decisions you're making during trial or right before trial. That is when your strategic direction has resulted in the creation of a pre-trial record, which then requires you to make tactical decisions about how you're going to use various parts of it.

Jeffrey Barist, Milbank, Tweed, Hadley & McCloy, Chair, National Litigation Group

It's a Matter of Facts, Not Just Theories

I have to confess that I generally find the facts of a matter more important than my most ingenious legal theory. The federal judge for whom I clerked my first year out of law school used to say: "Finding the law is easy (with an implication that even I was capable of that); it's finding the facts that is difficult." I think he was right.

One must begin with an understanding of the facts, and litigation in the American system is overwhelmingly fact-driven. The development of the facts, often in excruciating detail, is the hallmark of U.S. civil litigation. I am sufficiently experienced and skeptical that I do not profess ever to know with certainty what "the facts" are, as that might be determined by some omniscient objective reality. I must, however, have confidence that the facts being put forward to support my client's case are eminently supportable and more likely than not true. Most importantly, the litigator must make certain that the facts are true, at the least true in the minds of those who will testify to them. The vision of reality to be urged by counsel cannot be based on untrue facts. A witness cannot say the light was red, when in fact the witness believed the light was green. Nor is it helpful to a client's case to put a witness on the stand who now wants to say the light was red if he had told others previously that the light was green, unless he has a very convincing explanation for the change of recollection. I must add that I have never encountered the ethical dilemma beloved by law professors of the party who insists on taking the witness stand to tell a story that his lawyer knows is false.

I am something of an amateur historian and I see the creation of the factual context of a case as similar to what historians do. In both a courtroom and in a good work of history, there has to be a backbone. There must be a point of view, and the relevant facts must be dealt with, as they exist. Obviously facts cannot be fabricated, but must be truthfully told, marshaled, and reordered; that is, putting them in the appropriate order that allows the listener or reader to understand the point being made in an effective way.

A good trial lawyer, like a good historian, also knows when to discard and what to emphasize. One of the lawyerisms that I continually excise from drafts given to me to review is the insistence on using the absolutely precise date in a rendition of facts. It rarely makes a difference that the contract was signed on October 15, 1998, instead of October 1998. Mentioning the precise date focuses the reader's mind on an irrelevant detail and distracts from following the development of the story. It also distracts from when the precise date may be important, for example, that the alleged breach occurred on September 12, 2001.

The historian, however, is not supposed to have a point of view dictated by a client; when that happens the historian is quite rightly accused of special pleading. The litigator, of course, is supposed to be doing exactly that kind of special pleading, the conscious rendition and choosing of facts so as to advance a client's interests. The facts must be put in order and in an order that allows for the drawing of implications that advance an argument or position that the litigator is espousing on behalf of his client. For the most part, one should only have to read the facts section of a brief to learn everything one should need to be convinced. If after the facts section one has not convinced the reader, the brief has failed in its purpose of presenting the party's position effectively.

The litigator's rendition of the facts has in it the element of art, and an art reflecting the particular vision of the lawyer. Art is creating order out of chaos, and that is very much what a litigator does. A litigator takes a chaotic situation and creates order from it. The created order imposed upon the chaos is the litigator's vision of the reality that he now has to convince someone to accept as true. The force and persuasiveness of that vision of reality is ultimately what the case depends upon.

In complex litigation, however, the facts come out in excruciating detail. The challenge for the litigator is to take these facts, simplify them, distill them, and have them support an appealing and persuasive vision. Sometimes this has been called the theme of the case. I prefer to think of it as a point of view, a coherent, uncluttered message that compels the conclusion that my client is right. A very long time ago, I adopted the view that in any case, and the more complex the more this rule applied, I had to be able to take the case down to the point where in the course of a 15-minute discussion with an intelligent listener, that listener would come away with an understanding of the issues in the case, my client's position, and at the least, a sense that my client was probably more right than wrong.

Martin Flumenbaum, Paul, Reiss, Rifkind, Wharton & Garrison, Co-Chair, Litigation Department

---

Revealing the Makings of a Great Litigator

I like to be the person the client comes to with the insurmountable problem, the bet-your-company case. I like the pressure of that kind of problem and the intellectual challenge of trying to come up with a creative solution to it.

What impresses me in other litigators is a creative approach to problems. As lawyers, we get few problems as to which there are exact answers to those specific problems. A lot of what we do is trying to come up with answers or strategies based on analogous situations. The ability to take something that has been done in the past and apply it to a totally different set of facts and theories separates the good litigator from the great litigator.

One of the things I notice immediately about a young lawyer is an ability to write. One of the hardest things for young lawyers to learn, right out of law school, is to write persuasively and clearly in the style of an advocate. I notice immediately when a young lawyer is able to do that. A good, concise memo that's persuasive, to the point, and answers the question—that will make me take notice.

The other thing I look for is a certain passion about the practice of law. Good lawyers are not practicing law just because they think they might make more money practicing law than doing something else. There has to be some internal drive to grow as a lawyer, to become a go-to person on cases. I have some incredibly superb young lawyers whom I don't hesitate to send to talk to clients if I'm unable to be there, because I know they have that passion and that drive.

Lawyers on my teams have to work as hard as I do. They have to feel the same kind of dedication to the practice that I feel. We're all dependent on one another. When I run a big case and have a fairly large team on it, we generally have weekly meetings so that everybody knows what everybody else is doing. I think it's very important that everybody have a sense of the whole, and not just of the slice of the case they're focused on. If they know only the slice, they'll miss things that will be important to the case. I regard these meetings as very important. I try to avoid hierarchical reporting layers so that I'm working directly with the associates on whatever their areas are. This way, I know what they're doing, and they know they can always talk to me and come to me with an issue.

In the end, though, you can't measure success differently than your client measures success. We basically perform services for clients. Success doesn't necessarily mean winning every time; it may mean minimizing a loss; it may mean getting a smaller jail sentence than would otherwise be the case. There are lots of ways of measuring success, but they all have to be measured through the eyes of the client and whether the client is content with the result.

Martin Leuk, Robins, Kaplan, Miller & Ciresi, Chair, Business Litigation Department

The In's and Out's of a Successful Litigation Lawyer

In a book about litigation and litigators, some examination of the role of a litigator is in order. We take for granted that one who is a skilled litigator is by all accounts prepared to step into the courtroom in any situation and deliver polished argument and examination, all to the end of effective advocacy before a court and jury. In reality, a practical division of sorts exists between courtroom lawyers. One category is in fact the litigator. The other, the trial lawyer.

The two categories are neither formal nor mutually exclusive. In fact, almost uniformly, great trial lawyers are also great litigators. On the other hand, litigation skills alone do not make a trial lawyer. The line of demarcation between a litigator and a trial lawyer lies in the trial lawyer's special talent, skill, and experience in the courtroom.

Litigation is popularly used to describe anything from soup to nuts having to do with the civil dispute resolution process. A litigator must necessarily be able to take a dispute, place it into litigation, and layout and successfully execute a strategy which allows his or her client the best opportunity to obtain a favorable resolution, either by way of settlement, disposition, or trial. Whether, of course, a particular strategy is ultimately successful, often turns upon the litigator's skill and creativity during the discovery process and the pretrial motion practice, both of which are the stock in trade of a litigation lawyer seeking to position the case for the most favorable disposition.

A trial lawyer, on the other hand, is someone who has achieved some level of mastery in the courtroom. That is a different set of skills than what is required from the litigator. The trial lawyer must first have an ease of command in the courtroom. Jury selection, opening statement, direct and cross-examination, and argument are the standard skill set of a trial lawyer. These skills cannot be obtained solely by engaging in the litigation process, nor by infrequent appearance in the courtroom. Rather, as with the mastery of a musical instrument, mastery in the courtroom comes with many hours of practice both in and out of the courtroom.

A great trial lawyer is also likely to be a great litigator. No matter how skilled in the art of the courtroom a trial lawyer may be, success or failure often turns upon the strategy employed, the quality of the execution, and the decisions made during the litigation process.

Characteristics of Successful Litigation Lawyers

Many law firms recruit by looking solely to a certain segment of the law school class. A survey of the backgrounds of a large cross-section of the highly successful litigation and trial lawyers would suggest, however, that academic success in law school is not necessarily the best indicator of who will be a successful trial lawyer. Rather, certain intangible qualities are necessary, including judgment, tenacity, drive, ambition, and some steel.

Of course, a certain level of purely intellectual acuity is required. Lawsuits involve many varied issues of commerce, technology, and business on subjects that the actors have all studied diligently in higher education themselves. The qualities of the successful litigation lawyer, however, go far beyond the intellectual side. First and foremost, a successful litigator offers good judgment, both to make wise decisions in preparing and positioning the case as well as in guiding the client to make wise decisions as how to conduct its business so not to conflict with the object of the litigation, and to make wise decisions involving the disposition of the case. All of this requires excellent judgment. As a litigation and trial lawyer, you are confronted with making decisions without knowing what the impact of those decisions are. You have to make a way that allows you to move a case forward towards your ultimate goal and allows you to adjust your judgment as your opponents raise new issues.

A second characteristic is tenacity. Litigation is in many ways akin to a competitive sport. Once the lawyer has evaluated a case and placed it into suit, his or her evaluation may change dramatically for the simple reason that there now exists an individual(s) on the other side, who is also smart, experienced, and tenacious, whose sole goal is to destroy the case. Successful litigation attorneys are characterized by an ability to maintain their objectivity while things are not going well and continue to fight for their client without allowing fear of losing to enter into their thinking. It means you are not going to give up in representing your client to the fullest. Together with tenacity is the need for a powerful work ethic. The most successful litigators are often the ones who simply outwork their opponents. In the final analysis, it is attention to detail during the litigation process that sets up brilliant cross-examination and arguments in trial.

Of course, having all the character traits is only one piece of the equation. One hallmark of successful litigation firms is the degree to which mentoring takes place on a formal and informal basis. Experienced, senior litigators must play a hands-on role with younger attorneys to hand down the wealth of knowledge needed to successfully litigate a complex case. It takes years of this type of mentoring to take a smart, tenacious individual with good judgment and transform him into a genuine litigator capable of evaluating the strength of a claim or defense, laying out case strategy, deposing and defending witnesses, and bringing the right motions at the right time to either posture the case for trial or win it outright in the litigation process.

Michael Feldberg, Schulte Roth & Zabel, Chair, Litigation Department

Becoming a Leader, Not Just a Litigator

One the first things you have to do to become a leader in the field of litigation is to watch great lawyers. There are a lot of great lawyers out there, and while you can't stylistically be somebody other than yourself, you can pick up things from virtually every case you watch. One of the most important things is being open to many different styles and being open to learning from other people.

Some critically important skills for a lawyer to have are persuasiveness, which is a function mostly of sincerity; endurance, because you're going to work really hard; and the ability to question everything you are told, because a lot of litigating is about doing things that are counter-intuitive—part of what we do is to essentially go against the conventional wisdom. At the same time, don't make arguments that are going to get blown out of the water; if there's a weakness in your argument, assume it will be exploited. If you don't have an answer, don't make the argument.

For me, the single most important aspect of persuasiveness is credibility—making arguments that you visibly and audibly believe in. If someone thinks you're going through the motions with an argument—if they think you're reading a speech, or going through rote arguments that you make in every case—I don't think they're going to be terribly persuaded by what you're doing. The critical fact, and what separates people who are very, very persuasive from people who are a little less persuasive, is that the folks that really have it are perceived to be saying things they really believe.

If you are willing to learn from other people, you'll find that one of the things that separates the great lawyers from the okay lawyers is the extent to which they appear to believe sincerely in what they're doing and what they're saying. Being sincere means that you've thought through the various issues, and you are able to communicate an honest belief in the arguments that you're making. That sounds simple, but it isn't. At the end of the day, the single most important thing is only making arguments that, at some level, you believe in sincerely.

Harvey Kurzweil, Dewey Ballantine, Chairman, Litigation Department and Member, Management and Executive Committees

Qualities of a Successful Litigation Lawyer

The first characteristic of a successful litigation lawyer is intense dedication to preparation. It's not possible for the person who is actually going to be on his or her feet to over-prepare. It's not an issue of having an enormous army of people—which may or may not be required—but rather an issue of whether the person who is actually going to be standing up in court has really paid the price in terms of personal preparation. A good example is whether you have, as the trial lawyer, devoted yourself with a single-mindedness of purpose, so that after a certain date you have basically done nothing except get the case ready for trial. You have to pay that price.

Other characteristics of a successful litigator are an ability to react well under pressure, and having an ego that is efficiently resilient so you can allow for the possibility that you may lose. If you don't have the guts to recognize that you may lose, you will never be in a position to win, because you will never have what it takes to take a case all the way. You have to be able to withstand having a bad day or having a result that is less than what you would have hoped for. You need to have an intense dedication to your craft, always wanting to do better than you did the last time. You need to be willing to make personal sacrifices so that you can be as prepared as you should be.

You have to be honest: Never cut corners, because sooner or later it will catch up with you and you'll get a reputation among judges and other lawyers that your word can't be counted upon. You have to be courteous: You want to keep, or maintain, the reputation that you are an officer of the court, and you take your responsibility seriously. Always treat people working under you as your colleagues, not as your employees. And an additional characteristic, something I'm not sure can be taught, is having an instinct for what matters in a case.

What separates the good from the great litigation lawyer is the ability to be an effective courtroom presence. I've seen a lot of great litigators who aren't great courtroom lawyers, and what makes a great courtroom lawyer—based on people I've observed—is an ability to think on one's feet, to not panic, to speak with clarity, and to be able to take a complicated set of facts and make them simple and understandable. One thing that also makes for a great courtroom lawyer is an amount of personal credibility that some people have and some people do not have. You have to be credible, both to the judge and the jury. Sometimes people come across as too slick, and not forthright, and that is generally a fatal shortcoming.

At the end of the day, it is the client's satisfaction that determines whether you have succeeded. There are situations in which you can try a case because a matter of principle is at stake, and money isn't the object; you can try a case where there is no principle at stake, and it is solely money which is the object; you can try cases that should be settled but one side or another is not being realistic; and you can try a case, and occasionally, settle it on a basis that is better than your original objective, because you've maneuvered the case into a good position. But what it all comes down to is whether the client feels that he or she has been well-served at the end. That's the measure of success.

Joseph A. Hoffman, Arter & Hadden, Partner, Chairman of the Corporate Securities Practice Group

The Art of Negotiating: More Than Making a Deal

One of my greatest strengths is the experience I have gained in more than 20 years of practice. As a corporate and securities lawyer during this entire period, I have represented large and small public and private companies, investment bankers, banks and financial institutions, venture capitalists and strategic buyers, and individuals in a wide range of transactions. These transactions include corporate finance and acquisition transactions, public and private mergers, spin-offs, stock and asset purchases, and all types of securities transactions, including public offerings by public companies to raise capital for acquisitions and initial public offerings (IPOs).

I enjoy the sense of accomplishment in successfully completing a transaction. A recent transaction involved a company that was buying another company in a $250-$300 million deal. The negotiations were progressing at a reasonable pace, but as the deadline approached, we literally were working around the clock to sign the deal within five days. It was not very pleasant at the time, but I felt a tremendous sense of accomplishment when my client was ecstatic that they achieved the deal they wanted in the time allotted.

In many transactions, the challenge of finding a middle ground on issues, being creative in solving problems, bridging different positions, listening to what people are saying, and trying to find solutions, while dealing with egos and emotions adds to the satisfaction of a job well done.

When representing sellers, there is often angst about third persons discovering that the subject company is for sale. The seller often prefers to keep the sale a secret until the last document is signed. CEOs can be egotistical and demanding. Negotiating means more that just making the deal; it also means dealing with all sides of the table, getting the representatives together, and making everyone happy and agreeable with the result. The goal is to reach a position that is realistic with terms and conditions with which both sides can live. In a previous transaction, a seller of a business would not negotiate certain terms of the deal until the documents were about to be finalized and signed because he hoped we would agree to his unfavorable conditions. When our client maintained its position, he finally relinquished and, because it would give our client the deal they wanted, we were instrumental in revising and documenting the amended deal. The seller was an extremely difficult person with whom to bargain, but to obtain the deal, we tolerated his difficult behavior, kept our eye on the goal, and completed the deal in our client's favor.

What it Take to Be a Great Deal Maker

A successful deal maker gets things done on time. Time kills deals. When situations linger, the parties involved may change their minds. A recent client we represented in an individual capacity was involved in a deal that was prolonged because the seller of the business wanted to postpone the deal for a few months to receive favorable tax treatments. Then the market crashed, and the deal never closed. The opportunity to sell at a good price was forfeited because of the one-month delay.

A successful deal maker gets things done, but sometimes the best deal is the one that does not get made. In the process of due diligence, sometimes unavoidable issues arise. In another earlier deal, the quality of the revenue of the acquisition target was not what we anticipated because of some questionable billing practices. We decided not to proceed with the transaction. Everyone was disappointed because no one likes a dead deal, but the CEO believed that the thorough due diligence and the decision not to proceed saved the company the $300 million purchase price.

A successful deal maker does not get lost in theoretical issues. The client needs protection, but the attorney must also be practical about possible consequences. A successful deal maker listens to his client and assumes his client's perspective.

Mark J. Macenka, Testa, Hurwitz & Thibeault , Partner and Chair of the Business Practice Group

What Separates Superb Negotiators from the Rest

In my mind, the most persuasive negotiators can clearly articulate the reasoning behind the point they are making, as well as acknowledge the concerns the other side has. They are willing to make a decision and concede points, but only after determining why it's not a big issue in the first place. The most persuasive negotiators hit all the issues – not only their own, but the other side's, as well – and explain why those concerns pale in comparison or, while acknowledging their importance, demonstrate why those concerns are satisfied through other provisions or protections. By providing a reasoned explanation or rationale for their position, then even if they then discount the concerns of the other side and point out why such concerns aren't sufficiently compelling, or why those concerns are satisfied through other protections, it tends to be easier to resolve than if they just flatly said no.

When a rationale is clearly articulated and is not dismissive of the other side's concerns, it becomes easier to arrive at a compromise that can satisfy the concerns of both sides. If you are able to identify the other side's real concern, then it becomes easier to offer another alternative for protection that is tailored to that concern, while still being able to give your client what they need. This skill goes back to having deep and broad experience in the subject matter of the deal and being in command of the various terms and alternatives that can be suggested as compromises, as well as the ability to be able to take a step back to understand what the other side needs.

Caution: Dozens of Moving Parts

It's important to identify the various constituencies within a client's organization and make sure they are properly prepared for what to expect. Management may actually be multiple constituencies. For example, the CEO, the CFO, sales staff, and engineering department may all have separate stakes and points of view. Another group to consider is the board of directors, where there can be multiple constituencies there as well. Venture-backed clients or venture-capital investors have one way of looking at things, and a corporate investor on the board, for example, may have a different set of motivations they bring to the table. You must also consider the client's other professional advisors, such as investment bankers and accountants who may play significant roles in the transaction.

We spend time getting our clients to tell us what is driving them in the particular transaction to better understand how active various constituencies may be in the deal. For example, if it's a merger, the board is certainly going to be active, and there may be an independent committee set up. We will need to sit down with them and find out their perspective and what is driving the basis for the deal in their minds. The dynamic of who is truly sitting at the table can vary greatly depending on, for example, whether it's a technology licensing deal or a large acquisition or sale of the company. Each of these constituencies also needs to understand the process and what to expect. Having a basic understanding and comfort level with the process helps them to buy in to the result.

You can't neglect basic preparation. There's always a document at hand – a term sheet you're negotiating or a merger agreement or a financing document – that you must be fully familiar with, as well as with the prior deals that either party has done, particularly if they are public. You don't want to make a statement, and then have the other side pull up a deal your client has already done that contradicts your position. Although there are certain ways to try to deal with the other side calling you on something, such as saying that the client's corporate policy has changed since the time of the cited prior deal, it's better to avoid the situation altogether.

An important strategy while negotiations are ongoing is to have key team players remain focused on identifying and developing alternatives to the deal at hand. Creating viable alternatives, which may simply be a clear willingness to go it alone, not only adds to your leverage in negotiations, but the possibility of following another path can also serve as a catalyst for generating a sense of urgency in the other side and moving the current deal forward more rapidly. Even if, in reality, viable alternatives are long shots or at very early stages, it is helpful to create the impression that the deal being negotiated is not your only alternative. Keep in mind that the lawyers, the investment bankers, or the judicious use of a board member, can be helpful in this process.

When negotiating, it is important to listen to what the other side has to say. In my view, it's important that everybody understands the business or legal needs behind each comment. Try not to use non-negotiables, because deals develop and evolve and the decision-makers you represent, whether or not they're at the table, can often come back and compromise on a point you may have pitched as being non-negotiable. If they want to negotiate, it undermines your credibility.

It is important to know when it's time to settle or give in on your position. Part of this is to realize the importance of listening and being aware of what is happening at the table. You learn a great deal from the negotiating tactics of the other side. Some negotiators are very straightforward and constantly look for compromises to help get a deal done. If they search out compromises nine out of nine times, and on the tenth time, they say that this point is established corporate policy and they can't negotiate it, you could look through prior examples of deals they have done and realize they have never given in on this point. If I've done my homework and pulled down the prior deals to the extent that they are publicly available, I can have an associate quickly look through and vouch that that is indeed the case.

Situations can escalate at times, and if, for example, the CEO at the other side of the table seems fairly set in his or her ways, you can take a break and discuss that dynamic with your client. You have to take the temperature of the other side at different times throughout the process and constantly suggest alternatives or compromises. That is when it's important to have command of the issues and a broad base of experience behind you, so you can constantly approach issues from different angles and suggest compromises or alternatives. If you continue to run up against the same point, and the other side is able to articulate a valid business or legal reason they need to stick on that point, then perhaps it is time to leave that behind and go forward. Again, you have to talk to your own client and understand whether it is something they can ultimately live with.

There are different methodologies for managing a deal, depending on whether it's a merger, a venture-capital financing, or a technology licensing agreement. It is important to make sure your support team is in place, not only across levels of seniority, but also across disciplines. You cannot underestimate the importance of specialists who know how their particular expertise fits into the overall deal, and who also understand their advice needs to be tempered by practical suggestions and business savvy tailored to the specific circumstances at hand. This approach enables the team to better provide comprehensive, integrated legal and business solutions.

Doing a deal involves not just the negotiations, but a lot of planning and execution with a myriad of details, as well. For example, in almost every deal heavy due diligence is needed to investigate whether, among other things, there are other material agreements that affect the transaction in important ways. It's critical to make sure you line up the team and that you have both business people and legal people who can do the due diligence and review the appropriate agreements. There are many, many moving pieces at this level as well, parts that involve not just the negotiations, but also bringing in tax or intellectual property or litigation people or other experts who act as consultants and strategic advisors, and it is important to make sure everyone is on the same page. When you have three dozen moving parts, you have to make sure all those parts are being moved down the field at the same rate, so you don't wake up, having finally struck a deal, and realize all these other pieces need to be put in place before it can get done.

Richard S. Florsheim, Foley & Lardner, Chair, Intellectual Property Department

Innovation Protection and Today's IP Lawyer

The aspect of intellectual asset management that most people think of as the role of the IP lawyer is getting patent protection for the company's inventions. The role of the IP professional in protecting a company's innovations should be much broader than this. The IP professional can add value by helping the company select *which* intellectual assets to protect, *how* to protect them, and *when and for how long* to protect them.

Decisions on which intellectual assets to protect are important because the costs of protection are high. Companies simply cannot afford to protect innovations that will have no economic value. Designing a set of metrics that assist the company in distinguishing innovations worth protecting from those that are not is essential to a cost-effective intellectual asset management program. Such metrics should take account of factors relating to the importance of the innovation to the company's core business. For example, how likely is it that this innovation will be included in our products? How valuable will this innovation be to us, in terms of our ability to either save costs or maintain or increase our prices?

The IP lawyer's role in helping a company decide *how* to protect an innovation is fairly straightforward. Decisions about whether to protect through a utility patent, a design patent, a copyright, or a trade secret are the stock in trade of the IP lawyer. The quality of protection to seek, however – particularly in the case of a utility patent – involves important tradeoffs of quality and price. Companies will often opt for lower cost – at the cost of some risk to the quality of protection – for their less important innovations, but will seek the broadest and strongest possible protection – a more expensive proposition – for strategically important innovations. Discriminating between the critical and the mundane requires a keen knowledge of the technology and the company's business strategy, as well as a good crystal ball to help predict the future!

Deciding *when and for how long* to protect innovations can also be a complex process. In the case of patent protection, obtaining patent coverage for a single innovation worldwide can cost tens of thousands of dollars. The cost of maintaining a patent in effect worldwide for the entire term available is also very expensive. For this reason, companies must make informed decisions about which markets are important for a particular innovation, and review those decisions periodically to see whether particular patent protection can be dropped in some countries.

We have found astounding how many companies – including those with highly sophisticated management in other areas – simply have no idea which patents they are using in which of their products. It will rarely make sense for a company to maintain patent protection for a feature it has removed from its product line. Without such a "map," it is very difficult to make intelligent decisions as to where to file or maintain the company's patents. Ideally, the company should maintain a database that allows the decision-maker to see at a glance which products incorporate the features covered by each patent, and what the sales of those products have been and are forecast to be in each country where patent protection is being sought or maintained. Of course, there are situations in which it might make a great deal of sense for a company to have patent protection even in countries where its sales are low –

for example, in a country where its archrival's manufacturing facilities are located or where the archrival's sales are very high.

Victor M. Wigman, Blank Rome, Partner and Head of the Intellectual Property Department

Balancing the Art and Science of Intellectual Property

One of the most challenging parts of intellectual property law, particularly in patent law, is dealing with scientists and engineers and having them communicate fully and clearly their ideas and inventions. Many times, scientists and engineers are very concerned about losing their rights and having other people steal their inventions. Creating loyalty and a bond of trust with them is very challenging.

Keeping up with new technologies can also be very challenging. To be a well-rounded IP lawyer, you have to have at least some knowledge of emerging technologies in electronics, Internet, software, and biotechnology. You have to have a strong technical background and strong legal training. You have to be well organized and be the kind of person who pays attention to detail and is able to focus on extremely complex technical and legal issues. As an overriding consideration, you have to have the ability to communicate complex technical issues to judges and laypersons in a way that is both understandable and persuasive.

Intellectual property law is a balance of art and science. There are two sides to the brain, the scientific side and the creative side. The most successful IP attorneys are those that have abilities on both sides of their brains: the ability to understand and define technical subject matter on one hand, and the ability to be creative and to describe intellectual property, to define it and communicate it, on the other hand. I have known many patent attorneys who are strong technically but who are not so creative and have difficulty in effectively communicating their ideas and concepts.

A successful IP lawyer has to have to have integrity, and that has to be communicated not only to your clients but also to your adversaries, and, obviously, to the court. Coming across as a person of integrity – a person who can be trusted and whose word will be kept – will go a long way to ensuring your success, not only with clients, but in courtroom settings, as well. I never overstate the facts; I never intentionally misstate the law; I try to communicate a feeling or an aura of trust and integrity. Tenacity and diligence are also extremely important. What I notice in a lawyer is the ability to create a work product – a patent application, a brief, or an argument of some sort – and the ability to effectively communicate those concepts, to clients, adversaries, or the court.

To become a leader or a partner, you first have to have that ambition. Some people are content to be followers. To become a leader, you have to want it, and you have to have the knowledge and experience, which comes from playing the game, from being involved over many years. Certainly to become a leader or a partner, you have to have the ability to attract clients. Obviously, that goes for any field of law, not just intellectual property law. You have to be able to instill in your clients a trust that you have the ability and the resources to solve their problems, to understand their problems, and to advise them effectively. They have to trust that you have the technical ability, the legal ability, and the team behind you. That all comes with experience. If you want to start your own practice, heed the advice my father, a small businessman, gave me when I was starting mine: "Don't expect to have your clients all lined up before you hang out your shingle." In other words, be prepared to take a risk. Put yourself out there. Put your name and reputation on the line.

You can describe success in many ways. Success is demonstrated by results you achieve for your clients in obtaining patents or trademarks or enforcing those intellectual property rights and prevailing in litigation. Or it can simply be advising clients more generally on how to identify and define their intellectual property and to organize their internal departments to best accomplish those results. You know you are successful when clients come to you for advice – and then rely on the advice you give them.

Paula J. Krasny, Baker & McKenzie, Partner, Intellectual Property Practice and Group Coordinator, Chicago

The Best Advice is to Keep on Learning

I am learning new things everyday, so I do not know if I have received my best bit of business advice yet. I really like working with my clients. I like working with businesspeople and watching how they think, negotiate, and solve problems. I also learn from other lawyers, especially those who have a style different from mine. I have worked with people who are very different from me, and as a team, we have been extremely effective.

The federal judge who swore me into the Illinois bar gave everyone in the room a great piece of advice. She stressed that we needed to "be civil to each other." In fact, I had a trademark/domain name infringement case a couple of years ago that was very heated. After the case had settled, I called my opposing counsel and thanked him for being a gentleman throughout the case. It makes the fight more enjoyable, and you can serve your client better if you and opposing counsel are on the same playing field and stick to the issues. As we know, that does not always happen.

I have some advice I can give to aspiring IP attorneys, especially those wanting to concentrate in trademark law: Understand your client's business. It is important to know the law. If you cannot apply it effectively to your client's business, you are not as effective a counselor as you could be.

Know your stuff. A lot of people out there are holding themselves out as IP lawyers because they litigated one case or filed one trademark application. You do not want to be in a position where the other side has a competitive advantage because you do not know what you are doing.

Brandon Baum, Cooley Godward, Partner, Intellectual Property Litigation

Make It Simple, Make It Successful

Patent litigation involves a variety of arts. One of them is the ability to distill a complex idea down into something that is easy to understand and digest. Cases often involve multiple patents, and I was typically assigned to one patent or a group of patents and asked to teach them to everyone else on the litigation team.

When I started as a patent litigator, I was often tasked with distilling the patent into a single picture or a visual metaphor. My first assignment, for example, was to analyze a very complicated telecommunications scheme, which I simplified to the metaphor of a light switch going on and off. This analogy was then subject to a group critique in which people would attempt to take shots at it, because if we were ultimately going to use the metaphor, we had to be able to concretely defend it, since analogies can often be turned against you. That was much harder to do than I had anticipated. It is very easy to talk about a patent using the terms of the patent or technology. It is much harder to bring it down to a simple, understandable level. You want to be able to actually plug your analogy into a brief or argument and allow the judge or jury to say, "Now I get it. Now I understand what this patent is intended to do, and now I know how I am going to construe the claims or determine infringement."

Coming up with a visual metaphor of technology seemed like a frivolous exercise at the time. I couldn't understand how we could possibly justify this as litigation preparation. Once I finally did it, however, and saw how difficult it was, I understood the exercise and why it was important. We used that picture in every brief we filed with the court, hammering the metaphor home. Our opponent complained we were over-simplifying their patented technology. But the patent was ultimately dismissed from the case because the judge agreed our product did not perform like the metaphor.

I have since incorporated that approach into my presentations to court. It is a distilling process – the stripping away of extraneous material to find the essential core. There is nothing like the satisfaction you get when you argue in front of a judge about your client's patent, your client sitting behind you, and you have submitted a brief that describes the issues so tightly, so succinctly, that the judge says, "Yes, counsel, I understand, the patent teaches . . ." and uses the words from your brief to describe the patented technology. You know you have won, because the judge has just characterized the invention in the manner in which you want him to characterize it. If you can capture an idea with a perfect description, it is hard for the judge to refer to that idea using other, less-apt words. Again, it is a feeling of immense satisfaction when you have divined the case down to its most essential element – the one for which the other side has no answer.

That divining-down process is an ability that extremely skilled patent litigators can bring to the table. Engineers or old-school patent prosecutors and litigators often want to talk about whether a claim term element has an antecedent basis, a lack of written description, or other arcane points. While patent practitioners might be interested in such topics, they are rarely the critical, dispositive issues that will decide the outcome of the case.

The Golden Rules of Patent Litigation

First, patent litigation is 10 percent law and 90 percent technology. The patent laws themselves are fairly finite. Although there are a few obscure issues, for the most part one can rather easily learn the body of law. The rest is the technology.

Secondly, if you do not care about learning new things and learning them in incredible detail, patent litigation is not a suitable practice area for you.

Third – and I hate to use the cliché, but it fits here – "Think outside the box." Many patent litigators rely solely on the classic, standard litigation strategies. You must bring a level of creativity to the profession, and you must look for opportunities to apply that to every case.

Sometimes it is hard to see where your creativity will come into play in a particular case, but whether you begin to question ownership of the patent or begin to look at some unusual area of art, there is always the opportunity to apply your own creativity. For example, I was attending the multi-party deposition of the sole corroborating witness to the date of invention. After my co-defendants completed a day-and-a-half of questioning, I finally got my chance at the witness. Honing in on an offhand remark the witness had made in an earlier answer, I was able to make the story unravel. He eventually invoked the Fifth Amendment, eliminating himself as a witness. After the deposition was over, his attorney snarled, "You must have been a prosecutor."

Stuart Lubitz, Hogan & Hartson, Partner

A Formula for Success

I approach patent law as a problem-solver. There may not always be a specific problem, but there is always an objective, and as such, there is an attendant strategy or plan which is very fact-, client-, and industry-specific. There is no magic formula: That which works in the garment industry, for example, may not be successful in the semiconductor industry; and that which works in the semiconductor industry may not be applicable in the software industry. Patent lawyers must therefore thoroughly understand the specific circumstances they are working under and the specific clients for whom they are working, since there is so much variation within the field.

One client may want to establish a monopoly position. Another will want to minimize the royalties it has to pay because it is a latecomer to the industry, and its biggest problem is its ability to put a product on the market without being beaten with excessive costs from pre-existing patents and royalties, damages, and design changes. Others will start out very defensive, wanting simply to minimize royalty payments and at the same time develop a five- or ten-year plan to change that direction and become more aggressive in their market.

The strategies and plans you develop will therefore be very dependent on a fact-intensive study of your client, your client's industry, and its particular situation and objectives. Success in patent law comes from first understanding all of the facts, then structuring a plan that is well-suited to your client, and then working and changing your plan as circumstances develop over the period of time that you're executing the plan. This formula applies to everything from the overall business strategy of a company to the simple, short-term objective of introducing a particular product to the marketplace. In addition, when developing a plan, it is critical to always involve the client and the client's technologists. You must then periodically revisit what you are doing, keeping them informed on progress, and consistently reviewing the business objective, the legal objective, and the budget. At the end of the day, if you are performing up to a level of excellence, you will succeed with the client and for the client.

Cecilia Gonzalez, Howrey Simon Arnold & White, Partner, Intellectual Property, International Commercial Arbitration and Litigation

---

Elements of a Successful Lawyer

Success as an IP lawyer can be defined in three parts. First, success comes from the recognition of your peers. In my area, if anyone is looking at a "337" case, my name will come up, so there's name recognition for me as a specialist in that area.

Success also comes from winning cases. This is not a "how you play the game" situation; you are in there to *win* for your client.

Finally, success comes in the form of client loyalties. When you have clients who will come back to you again and again with their intellectual property problems, you build relationships with them, and you become an integral part of that company's business. Then, intellectual property is a very important part of their business. You are a player there, and you're the person responsible for helping them protect their property.

You can see some common traits of success if you look at a cross-section of successful intellectual property trial lawyers: A love for the technology and a delight in the constant learning and surprise elements of the technology with which we're dealing, combined with solid litigation skills. And there's an element of talent involved, as well. Some people are just very good – they walk into a courtroom, and they are *on,* like a light bulb goes on. If you combine that with the technical understanding and hard work, that's the winning combination. Those are the successful intellectual property lawyers.

I once had an older lawyer tell me most clients hire lawyers they can identify with, that they see a part of themselves in that lawyer. And I believe most people, when they are looking at a lawyer, want to see someone they think will be straightforward, honest to a fault, but willing to fight the fight to the very end on their behalf. The loyalty and service components are so important.

I think clients also want a lawyer who knows the law and who understands the area you're going to be dealing with. I believe people like to think of themselves as being prepared, so there's a projection element.

Dean Russell, Kilpatrick Stockton, Chairman, Intellectual Property Group

Intellectual Property Law in Context

My succinct description of the art of intellectual property law is that it is largely the development, perfection, and realization of assets that are born of ideas of the mind.

When I think of intellectual property, I think of assets: value added because of someone's idea. To the extent that there is an art to it, it's getting the value of that idea realized that forms the art of intellectual property law, and for that matter, intellectual property creation in general. The key is what you do from the genesis of the idea to make it have value, and from there you get into a whole host of issues that have legal implications: How do I use the legal system to make the idea have value? How do I make it have market and commercial applications? How do I make my idea into something salable, and salable at an appropriate margin? There are political issues as well: How do I make my idea salable at an appropriate margin without offending any segment of the market?

One of the most challenging aspects of IP law, which also provides one of the greatest opportunities, is that even today, the concepts of IP law are not especially well or comprehensively taught in the business schools of the country. So educating executives as to what IP and the legal system can add in terms of value is probably the greatest challenge. Many executives do not have background knowledge or a contextual framework of what IP law is all about. So the steep educational curve presents a number of challenges, particularly with harried executives who don't have or are unwilling to commit the time to learn about intellectual property. On the other hand, it is quite an opportunity if you can get executives focused on IP and IP law and help them understand at least the rudiments. I think then you have a much greater chance of success in realizing the value of ideas and having the companies that the executives deal with achieve their commercial success.

In intellectual property law, it's important to remember that where you are at any given point in time is not necessarily where you will be later on – a version of "what goes around comes around." Always think about what might happen in the future as a consequence of the action that you're taking today. What one company can do with intellectual property law, for example, its competitor can do just as easily. Anything that a particular client or I may do needs to be thought about in the context of what it will cause to occur downstream, particularly among competitors. In some situations, new technologies may develop for a period of time with no patents issuing. Simply acting to get the client a patent may cause competitors to spend more time and effort of their own in getting patents and ultimately cause the client difficulties down the road. All of that needs to be borne in context. So the golden rule of intellectual property law is to think of each of these actions in terms of what it may cause for the future.

Bruce Keller, Debevoise & Plimpton, Partner, Head of Intellectual Property Litigation

Components of Success in IP Litigation

One of the best pieces of advice I ever received was from a senior and very successful lawyer I met very early in my career, who told me to start every day by reading the newspaper. He was trying to impress upon a young lawyer just out of school that it was important to understand what is going on in the marketplace and in the world. He was, of course, quite right and his advice, updated for 2002, would be not only to read a major daily newspaper, but also to use the Internet to cull relevant information from a variety of sources. You need to understand marketplace developments to paint a clear and comprehensive picture for your client in connection with the issues for which they seek advice.

Another important lesson I learned early on is that you have to be willing to say, "I can do this. I know about this area. Let me tell you what my skill set is." That is hard to do, especially for a younger lawyer, because early in their careers they are unknown. However capable they may be, it takes time to convince potential clients to engage you because of these capabilities. You cannot be content to rely solely on the reputation of your firm if you want to establish your own credentials. Every lawyer should look at himself as somebody who ought to be identified as a leader of the bar. When you are young, it is hard to do that other than by performing great work for your clients on any assignment you are given. But you need to go beyond that and create a reputation for yourself as someone who is knowledgeable. Create an image for yourself that is consistent with, but separate from, the firm you are associated with.

You constantly have to make sure you are current and perceived as current. That is why I continue to give presentations, make speeches, write articles, and volunteer in ways large and small that give my firm and me exposure as a place to come if you have issues relating to intellectual property law. There is no substitute for going out and doing these things. You have to be active. You can't rest on your laurels because others will be glad to step into the vacuum you've created.

If you take care of short-term goals, long-term goals are more likely to be achieved. I did not sit down 20 years ago and say, "I will become a well-known intellectual property lawyer by the year 2000." I instead sat down 20 years ago said, "If I am going to be recognized as someone clients will want to come to, I need to establish credentials. What are the best ways to do that?" I immediately focused, therefore, on writing the next article, giving the next speech, making the next presentation.

William H. Brewster, Kilpatrick Stockton, Managing Partner

Secrets of Success in Litigation or Negotiation

For any lawyer, the ability to listen is essential to success. Listening is the first step: If you do not hear the information, you cannot do anything with it. The next step is the ability to apply real-world, practical knowledge to the situations you are handling. For example, I deal primarily with trademarks and brands, so understanding the marketplace, how products are sold, and how consumers receive information from advertising or messages in a supermarket provides critical background to the advice I convey to clients. It is extremely important to have a very strong, practical business side to your experience. Later, your ability to identify key facts and issues and then effectively convey that information to a client, the opposition, a judge, a jury, or whoever your audience is, will benefit from that practical knowledge.

I have done a lot of litigation, but I have also done a great deal of counseling, conflict resolution, and negotiation of agreements. If success in litigation means being able to prevail in a trial, you need two things: a client who has a stomach for litigation, which requires a large amount of time and money, and stubborn lawyers on the other side. In most cases, you do not get a chance to win at trial, because the matter ought to be settled before that stage. Clearly, if a case does go to trial, having good facts is critical.

In terms of negotiation, I try to put myself in the other side's shoes. After I have thought through our position and our perspective, I will make that leap and imagine what the other side is seeing and hearing. Whether you are negotiating an agreement or trying to settle a dispute, the biggest problem is not understanding the other side's concerns. I do the best job I can to figure out what factors are influencing them. If I have a hard time figuring out their motivations, then I will do my best to figure that out over the course of a negotiation.

If you can put yourself in another person's shoes – whether you are dealing with a witness, a client, or the opposition – you tend to be able to defuse arguments. If you can say to the other side, "I understand what you are saying; now let me get you to put yourself in my client's shoes," you will make progress. You don't have to say to them, "You are wrong. I am right." You can just demonstrate to them the difference of opinion or reasoning that needs to be brought to bear.

Being persuasive is about credibility and honesty. If you are in court, trying to persuade a judge, you hope to have a reservoir of goodwill based on being forthright and honest with the judge. If she asks you a question, you answer it not only as an advocate, but as an officer of the court. You explain there are two sides of the argument, and while you argue in favor of one side, you must be honest. The same principle holds for the opposition: If you mislead them during a stage of a negotiation or while in litigation, then your ability to be persuasive later – in settlement discussions or otherwise – will be destroyed. Obviously, your clients need to trust you, and your ability to persuade them to follow one course as opposed to another depends on their trusting you.

Mary B. Cranston, Pillsbury Winthrop LLP, Chair

Greatness Begins With a Vision

The more I have been involved in the law, the more I have come to view it as a service that allows our society and culture to work. The law is a set of ground rules that keep the economy going and our criminal justice systems working, and the lawyers, who are experts in these rules, are there to assist the society and culture in getting business done.

From my experience, one of the critical steps to becoming a great lawyer is developing a strong vision for yourself. This vision is so individualized that each lawyer needs to decide what being a "great lawyer" means to her or him. Once lawyers have established their vision, they go a step further: They do what they need to do to get there. This inner drive is the most important quality of a great lawyer. You need to decide what you want to do and where you want to go in your career. Picture yourself having achieved that vision. Keep this picture of yourself in mind with every decision you make, even the minute-to-minute decisions that seem minor or insignificant at the time. If you are clear about where you want to end up, you will end up there.

Great lawyers also recognize that people contribute in different ways; they work to figure out what their own strongest attribute is and how to capitalize on that attribute. For example, you may have a great mind for putting details of the law together, or you may be particularly skilled in how you tell the story to the jury. I believe each person is brilliant in several ways, which is why it is important to set your own goals. If you discover what you do better than anyone else in the world, you have found your niche. Then you can go for it to achieve your vision.

Certainly becoming a good lawyer involves some aspects of basic talent. There is a technical side to being a lawyer, which takes a lot of discipline and study to achieve depth and understanding of the specific rules – how they interrelate, where the gray areas in the rules are, and what the policy implications are behind the decisions made. Then there is the art, which is putting all of that together in a way that can be understood by your clients and by the non-clients you are trying to persuade. The art has to do with a person's ability to read situations and people, think creatively, and demonstrate advocacy skills. Again, developing these skills comes down to the commitment of the individual. A great lawyer has worked to hone all of these qualities, mastering both the science *and* the art.

Let me expand somewhat on the art of negotiating. Negotiations come down to understanding where everybody is coming from. That often requires you to drop your own blinders and try to put yourself in the shoes of the other person. Whether it is a contentious negotiation to try to settle a lawsuit or a more creative action where you try to come up with a new deal structure, the first and most important thing is to understand where the other person is coming from. It is also very important to always be honest and straightforward – although that does not mean you put everything on the table at the beginning. Further, it is also important to keep your own emotions out of the negotiation process. The discussion should be kept on an even keel emotionally. A lawyer's most important quality for winning a case is an ability to articulate the client's perspective in a way that is both legally correct and emotionally true. That requires a good set of advocacy skills, optimism, and an ability to clarify where you are going in the proceedings, whether before a court or a jury.

In addition to establishing your vision and developing your skills, you also must adhere to some absolute requirements you cannot violate as a lawyer. One requirement is that you uphold ethical standards. You also have to be straightforward, be courageous, tell your clients when there is a problem, and confront conflicts. Those qualities are absolutely essential. I believe very strongly in this, so I will say it again. Every lawyer, no matter what, needs to be a complete straightshooter.

I do not believe there is one correct way to be in terms of personality, or that only certain kinds of people make effective lawyers. I believe you can be a brilliant lawyer and be very kind. Whatever your particular package of skills, intelligence, and intuition, you can be a good lawyer if you really want to be. Although you may initially need to take some time to figure out what kind of law is appropriate for you, you will find your area. With regard to other lawyers around me, I respect high-quality legal thinking and the ability to take a set of facts and laws and make a difference by developing some new, creative win-win plan in litigation or business. I respect and require integrity. I also respect compassion and kindness.

How to Define Success

Law school is just the beginning of learning the legal skills you need to become a successful lawyer. Finding the best way to develop your skills depends on what you want to do. If you want to be a litigator, you would be well served to watch what goes on in a courtroom. Choosing a law firm that is committed to providing its lawyers with excellent in-house training and mentoring is also helpful. Years ago it would have been possible for young lawyers in big firms to get their trial skills by doing "slip and falls" for major clients, but those kinds of cases are not handled in big firms anymore. Today and in the future, young lawyers have a better chance to develop skills through an in-house university that allows lawyers to study trial skills, get practice, and place themselves in simulated situations.

On the business side, much of the training still comes from working with experienced lawyers, although attending as much backup classroom training as possible is also a good idea. If you want to become a sophisticated lawyer, you will probably need to go to a big firm right out of law school because they have the resources to train you and probably the clients and cases that are cutting edge. I expect this to be the case in the future, too.

I am frequently asked by new lawyers from just about every practice area how they can develop the timeless skill of persuasion. In courses taught in law school and elsewhere, you can learn about the skill and observe people who are very good at persuasion. But developing the skill takes time. Once you enter the work environment, you will see people who are effective, and you can watch what they do and try to imitate it. Borrow from these examples, and tailor what they do to your style. These skills do develop with time; I was not a very good public speaker when I started, but I was committed to learning from other people. Eventually, I grew into my public speaking style and now feel comfortable speaking in front of a variety of audiences.

I am also asked about how to develop intuition. The key here is to watch people who are gifted in terms of reading people well. You can watch how they handle situations, and then practice the skills you've observed.

No matter what kind of law or size of firm interests you, you will ultimately be responsible for your growth. So, to figure out what training would best help you achieve your goals, you will need to do your homework; never assume someone is looking out for you. Very importantly, you need to commit deeply to lifelong learning and work to strengthen your skill sets throughout your career. This will help you and your clients.

The definition of success is probably different for each individual. Most lawyers would agree on some things that success includes: bringing a high-value job to your client, getting the results the client wants and needs, working with the client to make sure the client understands what the law can and cannot do, and ending up with a situation where the client is satisfied and justice is done.

There is a distinction between personal success and success for the client – which most good lawyers work to define with the client. It is very relationship-specific.

To help grow our lawyers' personal and professional success, we have "full commitment plans" that people complete annually. The plan is basically a statement about what the lawyer aspires to accomplish that year. It is reviewed by the management of the firm at the beginning of the year, so we have a pretty good dialogue with every partner about what we expect and what we would like them to do, and we also hear from them about what they would like to do. We have the firm organized to meet client needs, so everyone works with a team to assess and meet our clients' needs. It is a very powerful device that allows lawyers in a non-threatening way to understand the clients' needs and sell themselves to the firm and to understand our business. Rather than telling our partners they need to go out and sell, which is a threatening notion to many lawyers, we give them a lot of support, and we have a very sophisticated marketing staff and knowledge management structure to help the lawyers understand what the clients are doing and where they are headed. This is a powerful set of tools to help our lawyers be successful. Finally, we have a very team-based culture. We do expect everybody to be their brother's and sister's keeper, and to help each other out. It is a great way to make sure lawyers succeed.

Advice from the Ages for Today's Lawyers

My grandfather, the CEO of a Fortune 500 company, told me this: "A business that is not recreating itself every day is dying." That was pretty insightful for someone who was leading companies in the 1960s and 1970s, and I think it is absolutely true.

If you want to be successful as a lawyer, you'll need to keep a few golden rules in mind. First, be absolutely straight with everybody in all aspects of your life. Second, remember that the clients are the most important thing, and your job is not just to accept as a passive vehicle your clients' demands, but to put your heart and soul into figuring out the very best thing for them. Third and finally, be compassionate to everyone.

Walter Driver, Jr., King & Spaulding, Chairman

Society and the Law: An Inextricable Relationship

Society must value the benefits we enjoy in this country because of the rule of law, as opposed to a political rule or a rule of dictatorship. The rule of law and transparency of process are keys to our democracy. Society must, by extension, also recognize the lawyer's role in preserving this system in which the rule of law reigns, so that the workings of the government are transparent to the people. To me, being a lawyer means serving clients in an independent manner; this provides the satisfaction of serving others in an intellectually gratifying way. This, I believe, is the primary function of the lawyer. We must all have stability in our daily lives and safety for ourselves, and in the United States, the rule of law is a bastion of preserving this safety and stability.

No matter how noble the law actually is, however, lawyers themselves many times come across negatively. Lawyers seeking publicity or personal gain for themselves, rather than the best outcomes for their clients, inevitably cause some of these negative impressions. Generally, the range of quality and personality you find in any large group of people, such as the American legal profession, is quite broad. Unfortunately, the stereotype in this field tends to emerge from the bottom of the barrel rather than from the top. It seems to me that both now and in the future, when a client needs you and you do a genuinely good job, they are very appreciative. That's success, even though they might be the one telling the next lawyer joke.

Bryan L. Goolsby, Locke Lidell & Saap LLP, Managing Partner

The Art of Being a Good Lawyer

Simply stated, the key factor in being perceived as a "good lawyer" by your clients is being recognized as bringing value to their business through focused expertise and outstanding service. To be considered a "good lawyer" in a law firm, you must be focused on the fundamentals of your practice – not only developing a reputation for expertise and top-quality work, but also developing the skills to have a rapport with your colleagues and clients. If you develop a reputation for doing your work right, doing it fast, and doing it with integrity, your productivity, your compensation, and ultimately your success, will naturally follow. There are no shortcuts to success in any service business, particularly the business of providing legal services.

Many new lawyers don't understand that the practice of law is not only a business, but it is primarily a "people business." To succeed in this business, you must not only communicate with your clients, but also interact with them in a manner that makes them recognize that you have unique expertise and that your interests are aligned with theirs. This perception is critical so that your clients don't view your legal services as a commodity. Being viewed as a commodity can result in a client comparing your rate and services with those of other lawyers, as opposed to appreciating the particular value you bring to a given transaction or matter. The art of being a good lawyer is being able to distinguish yourself from other lawyers through more than just technical ability.

The difficulty for law firms in recruiting attorneys out of law school is the inability to accurately gauge the intangible qualities of a potential lawyer. While most firms focus on a candidate's academic record, this is only an indication of how good a lawyer may ultimately be from a technical standpoint. Without question, if you're not a good technical lawyer, it's hard to become successful. But technical skills are only a small part of the equation necessary for success. If you cannot translate that technical ability into a client's feeling of confidence, it will be difficult to be rewarded by that client for the value you may be bringing to his matters. To some extent, the difference is not how good a job you did, but how good a job your client thinks you did. Marketing your expertise and your results to a client are not skills taught in law school, and it's something many lawyers have difficulty mastering. How a client perceives value is a key ingredient in any attorney's success.

A law firm's total performance is based on its attorneys performing high-quality work and being paid appropriately for those services. The challenge is not only delivering a high-quality product to a client, but also giving that client an incentive to send you additional work in the future. Assuming a quality result, service may be the determining factor in getting additional business.

In law school, time is your friend, and you can, if necessary, stay up all night to study for a test. Time is your enemy when you're a lawyer. You often do not have the luxury to devote an infinite number of hours to a particular project. Multi-tasking is essential. You have to be able to work on a variety of different projects at one time without affecting a client's perception of the importance of their particular project. Even though your workload may be overwhelming, you cannot afford to let it affect the quality of your work or your service levels. The ability to perform numerous tasks efficiently it not so much a strategy but a requirement.

Robert F. Ruyak, Howrey Simon Arnold & White, Managing Partner and Chief Executive Officer

The Steps to Success in Litigation

If you concentrate on litigation and trial work, the "art" is understanding how people think, how they react, and how they use their life experiences to make decisions. The entire goal of a trial is to persuade a jury or a judge that your client's position justifies their decision in your favor. If you have a sense of how people think and how they operate, you are more likely to be able to persuade them.

There are several characteristics of successful trial lawyers. The first one we have just addressed – understanding how people think, feel, and operate. You must have good judgment about human nature – not just any human nature, but the particular nature you are dealing with. Judges are often very different from jurors, for example.

Second is the ability to tackle and master new and unfamiliar information. The ability to synthesize and use complex facts to persuade your audience can vary dramatically in terms of difficulty, depending on what kind of case you're working on. Having a complete command of the facts will be persuasive. Most people – most Americans, at least – are persuaded by the facts and the circumstances that they learn or infer from a particular argument or position. The facts can include the documents involved, oral historical detail, and the people and personalities involved. Some of the best trial lawyers can almost block out nearly everything else and absorb enormous amounts of information in a very short period of time, and then synthesize it and play it back in a way that is understandable and persuasive. You cannot be superficial; you must have depth and breadth in your understanding of the subject matter. Being persuasive is not simply spouting off favorable facts. Persuasion is confronting what your opposition or a witness says by taking individual witnesses' testimony and documenting evidence and putting it together in a form that is convincing.

The third characteristic is simply a broad life experience. Some of the best trial lawyers I've met are people who have had a variety of experiences. They've had the opportunity to work with different types of people from different economic and social levels. When you do that, you have a better understanding of how people think, react, and feel. Armed with that knowledge, they understand the appropriate way – indeed, the persuasive way – to approach their audiences.

Organization is the fourth essential ingredient of success. You need to arrange the evidence that proves your client's position in an organized fashion. Juries use common sense as a principle method of evaluating what they see and hear. That does not require being pedantic or practicing law in a textbook way. It means being able to sense what is important, choosing your issues wisely and supporting your position with facts organized in a deductive sequence – one that a judge or jury is most likely to understand and agree with.

Success is not likely without the fifth characteristic: time commitment. Achieving success as a trial lawyer requires an extraordinary amount of time and an intense concentration on the case. You need to have a great deal of patience and be willing to be consumed by the facts. Most people are convinced when they believe that the speaker knows what he is talking about. You must convince the fact-finders that you have complete command of the facts and have thoroughly analyzed them, and that your arguments are not conjectural, but are the true and proper conclusions.

Timing is Everything

The successful practice of law is time-intensive; the challenge is managing your time effectively. You have to devote a tremendous amount of time to understanding and capturing what you need to know to be persuasive.

Related to this is the challenge of balancing personal and professional lives. Some people get caught up in the belief that clients and the firm demand all of your time, but I've never subscribed to that view. Many lawyers make the mistake of devoting their entire lives to their practice. Quite frankly, those people are successful only to a point. When they fail, they lose perspective and burn out. The practice of law is a job; it's how you earn your income and provide for your family. But it should not be the primary goal of your life. I've always reminded myself, "You need to be able to walk away from it." I think people have to be prepared to do that. As a practical matter, it requires time management skills and the ability to delegate responsibilities. For me time management is ironclad – I plan my schedule so I have significant personal time with my family, and I don't allow interruptions. Admittedly, being in litigation makes this difficult because judges and clients constantly want your time. But I have always found that if you set limits, people will respect them.

A second challenge is simply dealing with people. In a litigation trial setting, you deal with witnesses and clients with emotional views on the issues – particularly in cases that involve hundreds of millions of dollars. Emotions and sensitivities lie behind the scenes. Witnesses' recollections, judgments, and demeanor can be adversely affected by them. One of the big challenges is being able to deal with personality traits and perspectives. You must gain witnesses' trust, help them recollect, and help them formulate accurate and objective testimony.

A third challenge is case management. With witnesses, attorneys, legal assistants, and support staff, you often have a considerable number of people helping you prepare for trial. Managing the case well, so the team can meet all the deadlines, marshal all the law and the facts, capture the right documents, prepare the key witnesses, and put the puzzle together is a huge challenge.

R. Bruce McLean, Akin Gump Strauss Hauer & Feld LLP, Chairman

Preservation, Representation, and Passion

Lawyers have two important sets of responsibilities. First, we are responsible for preserving the rule of law. Our system is based on the expectation that lawyers will conduct themselves in an ethical and responsible manner, and with a high degree of integrity. Absent this integrity, our entire system would collapse. Second, we must vigorously represent our clients as advisors and advocates. Our system of justice demands a high level of advocacy to reach a just result. Balancing these two responsibilities can pose enormous challenges.

Being a successful lawyer is more of an art than a science. All lawyers are grounded in the science of reading and understanding the law, whether it is statutory law or the interpretation of case law. The art is in the application of the law to ambiguous facts and messy circumstances. Whether you are a litigator or a corporate lawyer, you must understand the client's situation, interpret and apply the law to the circumstances that present themselves, and achieve a result that is consistent with your obligations as a lawyer and provides your client with an optimal result.

A successful lawyer combines both the art and the science of being a lawyer. A successful lawyer effectively uses his intelligence, has first-rate communication skills, possesses a high level of motivation, is grounded in a sense of integrity, and exercises sound judgment to achieve the very best results for the client at all times – and enjoys the task, for a lawyer who is passionate about his or her work is a successful one. He or she shows respect for clients, colleagues, and adversaries alike.

Measuring and Building Success

Extremely successful lawyers exist in all areas of legal practice. Such lawyers have certain key characteristics in common, including intelligence, excellent communication skills, a very high degree of motivation to serve their clients well, integrity, and sound judgment.

The ability to relate well to people is critical. Successful lawyers can communicate with people and gain the confidence of not just their clients, but everyone with whom they work.

Judgment is a critical factor that separates a good lawyer from a great one. Many lawyers are intelligent and analytical, and therefore have the ability to gain a thorough understanding of the law. But effectively applying the law to the disorderly and sometimes chaotic world in which we work requires judgment. Sound judgment is born of instinct and the intuitive ability to sift through the various aspects of problems and devise creative solutions. It matures as we gain experience. Sound judgment is vital to study a very complicated problem, make the best decision, and provide the client with the correct advice. Take a look around the country at successful lawyers at every level, and you will notice the one thing all successful lawyers have is absolutely sound, unerring judgment.

A high degree of integrity also is essential. Successful lawyers are those whose word can be trusted and whose representations are true and complete. Lawyers lacking integrity will find this shortcoming will catch up with them. I have seen many great lawyers practice, and every one of them represents the highest standards and ethics in the profession.

To help our lawyers achieve success as we've defined it, we must mentor them. Leading by example is one of the best forms of mentoring. Successful and accomplished lawyers must work with younger lawyers to develop the skills that will be necessary to make these young lawyers great. Mentoring is a vital part of what we do in our firm, and a very important part of how good lawyers get to be great lawyers. It is unusual for a lawyer to become a great lawyer strictly by his or her own instinct, talent, and experience. All great lawyers have mentors.

Some lawyers – whether they'll admit it or not – measure success by the number of clients a person represents and the amount of money he or she can earn. That is a poor measure of success. Certainly, many successful lawyers have a substantial client following and make a great deal of money. Yet far more important than earning a significant income is making a difference for our clients, within the legal system or in society as a whole. This is the true measure of success.

Jack H. Nusbaum, Wilkie Farr & Gallagher, Chairman

Staying On Top of Your Game: It's an Art Form

Part of the art of being a good lawyer is listening to your clients' problems, understanding their goals, and helping them reach those goals. Being fully conversant with the facts and the problem at hand is another part of it – but the most critical issue is being responsive to the clients and making them feel nothing is more important to you than the particular problem you are working on with them.

With regard to the science of being a good lawyer, understanding the legal problem is a good start. If you can spot the issue and understand it, you can then do the research necessary to understand the precedents and how you can apply them in a particular situation. So the science is really understanding the problem, doing the research carefully, and then convincing someone that your side has the better argument. It is always the same task: proving your side is more right than wrong. The side with the better command of the facts and the law will always win. That is the scientific part.

Hard work is the most important element in winning a case, and you also need the facts in your favor. More often than not, the facts will dictate the result, but in those instances where the facts are even on both sides – and some cases are like that – then the person who works harder, is more creative and thoughtful, and devotes more time and energy to the case will probably prevail.

To make sure you are on top of your game and that you appear that way in the courtroom, the best strategy is to just study the facts and study the law. If you know both and you have them at your fingertips, you will be on top of the game. I do not travel with an entourage or several briefcases. If you take the time beforehand to put the information that is in those boxes into your head, you do not need any of that. You come with a pad, a pencil, and a head.

The most important part of a negotiation is understanding your end game. Before you go into a negotiation, you have to know what is important to you and your client and what is important to your counterpart and his or her client. You have to navigate the channels to allow both sides to achieve most of their objectives, because a successful negotiation is never where you get everything you want and the other side gets nothing. You want to give up what is not important to you, and keep what is important to you. Preparation for that negotiation is every bit as important as the negotiation itself.

I have always found that yellers and screamers are the least effective negotiators. People who speak quietly, forcefully, and intelligently are most effective. Also, talking too much in a negotiation is not good because eventually you become white noise. People who do not talk much, but have something relevant to say when they do, often turn the focus of the meeting toward what they are saying.

Good and great lawyers both have all the skills needed to be successful. Separating good lawyers from great lawyers sometimes has to do with exceptional intellect. Some people are so smart that they stand out from the rest by virtue of their intellect and thought process, but those are few and far between. More often it is the intangibles – the art of being a lawyer, of persuasion, understanding, and being able to convince a third party of the correctness of your position. No matter how strong your case is or how brilliant your mind is, if you cannot translate that brilliance either to the written word or to the oral word in negotiation in oral arguments in a court, you will not be a great lawyer. The really great lawyers can marshal their facts and the law to make a persuasive argument.

Going to the best schools always gives you a leg up, whether it's the best law school, the best college, or the best engineering school. However, many of the best lawyers did not go to the best law schools. That is only the beginning. You have to take advantage of the education you receive. The element the top law schools provide you – and actually all law schools do if you pay attention – is to teach you how to think like a lawyer. Lawyers are different from artists because artists can be conceptual, and lawyers have to operate within the four corners of the law. Thinking like a lawyer, spotting the issues, and understanding what is important and what is not are some of the key successes that have to be achieved for young lawyers early in their careers, when they are actually doing the legal work. It is really a question of learning to think like a lawyer and then applying that learning to the actual task.

Keith W. Vaughan, Womble Carlyle Sandridge & Rice PLLC, Chair, Firm Management Committee

How the Lawyer Should Define Success

Any effort to address the art and science of being a successful lawyer must begin with a clear understanding of the term "success" as used in the context of attorneys practicing their craft. Much has been written in recent years about the business aspects of practicing law. Concepts such as "leverage," "client and matter profitability," and "commodity work" are as much a part of the vocabulary of attorneys in mid-size and large firms as the familiar legal phrases *"stare decisis"* and *"res ipsa locquitor."* A casual review of today's legal publications might, therefore, prompt the reader to conclude that a "successful lawyer" is one who employs that set of business practices which generates the greatest profit. Although any profession should seek to employ effective business strategies whenever possible, the true measure of an attorney's success has little to do with the financial consequences of a particular matter for the individual attorney.

Success as a lawyer is properly evaluated according to such standards as the quality of the effort expended by the attorney, the extent of the service rendered to the client, the degree of professionalism displayed throughout the life of the transaction or legal proceeding, and the extent to which the attorney uses his talent and skills to serve others. This chapter identifies the characteristics of a successful attorney as measured by these criteria and concludes with additional suggestions for those who wish to be successful practitioners in a mid-size or large firm.

Characteristics of a Successful Lawyer

Commitment to Client Service

All successful attorneys have one characteristic in common: They are absolutely committed to client service. They may come from different law schools. They may have chosen to specialize in different areas of practice. They may vary in legal knowledge and skills. They may differ in age, gender, race, religion, or background. But, in the final analysis, all are devoted to their clients and are motivated by an overwhelming desire to serve their clients' interests. The flipside is also true. Highly skilled attorneys who are not committed to serving their clients will achieve only temporary success at best. As one of my partners said recently, "Clients don't care what you know until they know that you care." The importance of this factor is not surprising when you remember that lawyers are in the business of providing professional (in our case, legal) services. The use of legal knowledge and skills *to serve* is the essence of what we do and what clients expect.

Client service is much more than merely a desire to be helpful. It involves transforming that motivation into action by focusing on what is in the client's best interests and then both establishing and accomplishing a course of action necessary to satisfy those interests. Each element of this process is important. Determining what is in the client's best interests requires going beyond a thorough inquiry to determine what the client is trying to accomplish and requires putting yourself in the shoes of the client but with the benefit of your own training and expertise. In other words, successful attorneys know their clients' needs and desires as well as their clients do and are alert to issues their clients have not anticipated. They can then assist their clients in developing strategies that fully accomplish their clients' objectives.

It is important to note that, in carrying out the "game plan," two aspects of client service are critical. First, the entire process must include frequent communication with the client. Too many lawyers, especially those fresh out of law school, focus almost exclusively on the end product – the memorandum, closing papers, or jury verdict – and regard the client as irrelevant, if not a distraction. Almost every client wants to be part of the process, and the lawyer ignores him at the lawyer's peril. From the client's perspective, it is usually impossible to distinguish one legal product from another, but it is quite easy to determine which attorney seemed most interested in being certain the client's needs were being met.

Second, the successful attorney attempts to exceed client expectations whenever possible. For example, she determines at the outset the length of time required to accomplish an action or series of actions and so advises the client. She then delivers the services or product *before* the expected date. Frequent communication with the client and consistently exceeding the client's expectations are key characteristics of a lawyer committed to client service.

The importance of a mastery of legal concepts and skills to anyone who wishes to be a successful lawyer is so obvious as to require little discussion. All clients expect their attorneys to know the law and to possess those skills necessary to perform the task at hand. The truly successful attorneys, however, are those whose mastery of legal concepts and skills are so complete as to allow them to achieve creative solutions to client problems.

No one can perform at this level upon leaving law school. Excellent law schools equip their students with fundamental legal concepts and a way of approaching legal issues that provide a foundation for a successful legal career. That educational framework must be followed by years of experience in applying the legal concepts to a variety of factual situations and the testing of various approaches. This experience must in turn be supplemented by continuous efforts at professional development to acquire additional knowledge and improve skills. The process is never complete. Successful lawyers first master basic legal concepts, then the specific laws and skills applicable to their areas of practice, and finally focus on being on the cutting edge of their specialties. There are no shortcuts.

Often overlooked in a list of the key characteristics of successful lawyers is an understanding of human nature. A lawyer who has mastered legal concepts and skills incident to his specialty but lacks this characteristic is simply a technician. Even if he is committed to client service, his chances of becoming successful are significantly limited.

Legal issues and problems do not exist in a vacuum. They arise out of relationships between human beings. Ultimate resolution of any dispute or completion of a transaction requires decisions by human beings, whether the resolution is by agreement or a legal proceeding. The greater the number of people involved in the development of the ultimate solution to the problem, the more significant are the human variables that must be addressed.

The importance of an understanding of human nature is even more obvious in the litigation context. From the moment a lawsuit is even contemplated, the successful trial lawyer is balancing a long list of such considerations. She must predict likely reactions to every conceivable strategy by the judge, jury, witnesses, opposing counsel, co-counsel, client, and, in high-profile matters, the press and the public. She must anticipate, as well, the potential responses of each of these individuals to the strategy of the opposing counsel and to the actions of anyone else involved in the proceeding. The process is dynamic and becomes the true focus of the successful trial lawyer. For some, this process is almost intuitive, but for many it is the result of years of careful observation of people in action.

The best way for any lawyer to approach the human factor in a litigation context is to begin work on any new case by focusing on the end of the case and answering a series of questions: What are my client's goals in this litigation? Who will be the decision-maker – trial judge, jury, appellate court, or opposing counsel (whom I hope to persuade to either throw in the towel or settle)? What will be the most persuasive arguments I can make to that party (or, in many cases, to those parties)? As I try to develop those arguments, what evidentiary or human resistance am I likely to encounter, and from whom? What strategies may I employ to overcome this resistance?

Then, she must step into his opponent's shoes and ask the same series of questions from that viewpoint. Only then can she prepare a strategy that allows her to make her most effective arguments for the decision-makers and prevent her opponent from advancing the opponent's most effective arguments. At all times she must remember that an argument is effective only if the decision-maker finds it to be so.

Every successful trial lawyer follows some form of this process in a disciplined manner. There is no substitute. The human elements of litigation are not just important – they are critical, and the successful trial lawyer knows it.

An important aspect of human nature that frequently comes into play is the difficulty of reaching rational decisions when emotions are high. Simply stated, a successful lawyer knows that neither he nor his client should make important decisions in a case or during the course of a transaction if either is especially angry, elated, disappointed, impatient, or frustrated as a result of a recent event. Almost invariably, the inclination is to be unduly generous or demanding, neither of which is likely to produce a favorable outcome for the client. Every transaction or trial yields one or more moments when emotions do not control the decision-making process, and it is then that the resolution of issues should be attempted. Likewise, the successful attorney is alert to the emotional reactions of his opponent that might produce opportunities for a favorable outcome and seizes those opportunities.

All of the foregoing considerations achieve maximum impact when the lawyer is an effective communicator. Unquestionably, all lawyers can communicate to some extent, and most do so far better than the average person. Somewhat surprisingly, however, many attorneys have never really mastered the art of communicating effectively in a variety of contexts. In recent years, attorneys in a number of large firms have commented on writing deficiencies they observe in new associates. The concern is not that these new lawyers struggle to write complete sentences. Rather, it is that many do not organize the material in a clear, logical way and take the reader through the material with appropriate transitions. Furthermore, they observe that the language used is not simple and direct. Any attorney taken to task over her writing style should take the criticism seriously and seek help immediately. A number of legal writing programs have surfaced in recent years, perhaps because of these concerns. An attorney must be able to write clearly and concisely if she is to be successful.

Of equal importance are oral presentation skills. Attorneys who are excellent public speakers have a significant advantage in almost every area of practice. Even those who are not called upon to address judges or juries find themselves sooner or later making presentations to boards of directors, business groups, or their peers. The quality of these presentations will influence those who are in a position to determine whether the attorneys will ultimately be successful. In addition, the presentation itself is almost always designed either to inform or to persuade the group to whom it is given; that is, it has a purpose. The purpose is rarely accomplished if the presentation is not effective; hence, an opportunity to succeed is squandered.

One other aspect of communication is important for the attorney who wishes to be successful: the ability to lead meetings. Attorneys frequently find themselves in legal, business, or community meetings, and almost as frequently are eventually afforded the opportunity to lead the group. Leading meetings effectively is an art form in itself, and few people do it effectively. Those who do assume greater and greater leadership roles in contexts that enhance their abilities to be successful. A short course on leading meetings is well worth the effort.

A successful attorney adheres to the standards and ideals of his profession. At a minimum, this involves practicing within the bounds of the law and the canons of ethics in his state. But it really means much more. To be truly successful, an attorney must gain and maintain the respect of his peers. He knows that to do so he must not only demonstrate his overall competence or even an extraordinary level of skill, but must also establish consistently that he can be trusted in all of his dealings with other attorneys and the public at large. Breach of that trust usually stains a legal career forever. To state the obvious, an attorney who proves not to be trustworthy is not trusted. Integrity is therefore the most important characteristic of a successful attorney. Without it, his individual "successes" have no meaning, and his purported commitment to client service is more properly viewed as a commitment to winning.

Integrity is simply a personal commitment to act honestly and honorably at all times, to be true to oneself, to do what is right, regardless of the consequences. In many ways it is an internal compass that automatically steers us in the proper direction without the intervention of outside forces. Acting with integrity is its own reward, but it also enhances the attorney's ability to be successful in any transaction or proceeding. A lawyer whose integrity is beyond question can obviously be trusted with far more significant matters than one whose integrity is in doubt. A successful lawyer's word is his bond, and he is treated accordingly.

Professionalism also includes the manner in which lawyers deal with each other. Successful lawyers treat their peers and others with respect. They do not need to belittle other people or humiliate them to be successful. They do not distinguish between their peers on the basis of race, religion, or gender. Their talent, skills, and commitment to client service are sufficient in themselves, and anyone they deal with knows it.

One of the greatest challenges a lawyer faces is allocating his time appropriately among a variety of different interests, each of which has a legitimate demand on his time. The old saying is, "The law is a jealous mistress." It means the practice of law can be an all-consuming task, leaving little time for other activities. To have a successful legal career, an attorney must find ways to achieve an overall balance in his practice and between his practice and life on the outside.

If one is committed to client service, this commitment alone can be a full-time job. Realistically, to survive financially, most lawyers must serve a number of clients simultaneously. The result is competing demands for the lawyer's time and a need to juggle these demands effectively. The art of the successful attorney is being able to represent simultaneously a number of clients on a variety of matters and do so effectively. The lawyer must develop proficiency in a number of areas to accomplish this task.

First, he must master the various skill sets I've already mentioned. His ability to juggle various matters simultaneously will be hindered by ineffectiveness in any of these areas simply because it takes longer to perform those tasks that one has not yet mastered. Failure to take the time necessary for each task is not an answer because the result will be negatively affected. In other words, one must take the time early in one's career to develop all of the necessary skills, so he can go faster later.

Second, the attorney must develop a satisfactory time management system. Various programs, books, and articles offer suggestions, and the key is finding what works best for the individual attorney. The most important points, however, are that there must be a system, and it must include a process for setting priorities among the competing demands.

Third, the attorney must control the demands on his time instead of letting the demands control him. The latter leads to frustration and occasionally depression or more serious consequences. Part of the solution is recognizing when the demands are overwhelming and help is needed. Under no circumstances should the attorney mislead the client or opposing counsel or the court about when a task will be completed or make promises he cannot likely keep. Such actions can lead to disastrous short-term consequences and, on a long-term basis, make the attorney less trustworthy.

In many ways a greater challenge is presented by the desire to balance career and family obligations. Each can make a strong claim for all of the attorney's time. At the same time, there is no direct confrontation between career and family. Both focus their demands on the attorney and look to him to resolve the competing claims. He must constantly remind himself that he alone controls his schedule, and he alone is in a position to make each party aware of his need to spend certain time with the other.

For example, the attorney should start by sharing with his family what he is trying to accomplish in his career. He should stress that practicing law is serving other people and that his doing so is valuable to society as well as his clients. He must make them see the value in what he is doing and share in his desire to serve others. At the same time, the attorney must demonstrate to his family by his actions that ultimately they come first. He should affirmatively seek out opportunities to be with his family and attend important events in the lives of his children. It is always easy to push aside a family event and fill it with a client activity under the theory that it is good for business or the client or even the family because of the potential financial rewards. Most clients, however, face similar conflicts and can both understand and respect their lawyer's desire to spend time with family. Frankly, if the client is unreasonably demanding in this regard, the attorney should avoid a long-term relationship with this client. Again, this balance is not easy to achieve, but it is difficult to consider an attorney successful if his personal life is in tatters because of his pursuit of his career.

People who go to law school are blessed with certain talents and skills that can be used to advance the interests of the community and the legal profession. A successful attorney finds time during the course of her career to serve both groups. The service can be through community or bar associations, one-on-one with people in need, or even through the political process. The opportunities for service are many, and the attorney can select the ones that appeal most to her.

Have we addressed all of the key characteristics of a successful lawyer? Consider them in combination and then decide by asking these questions:

Can anyone seriously argue that an attorney is not successful if she is committed to client service, has mastered legal concepts and skills, understands human nature, communicates effectively, conducts herself in a professional manner, effectively balances competing client and family demands, and serves her community and profession? Can anyone seriously argue that an attorney is truly successful if she lacks any of these characteristics?

The answer to each is obvious. One final question might also be asked: Would the answer to either of these questions change if the attorney were financially successful? Of course not. Techniques for increasing the profitability of a legal practice are valuable from the standpoint of improving a lawyer's financial status. They do not, however, define a successful legal career.

Alicia Abell, Author, *Business Grammar*

Top Seven Tips for Effective Legal Writing

1. Know why you're writing.

Before you begin writing, know what you want to say—and why you want to say it. Are you explaining a situation or a problem? Are you trying to convince the reader of something? Are you recommending a course of action? One way to ensure you know why you're writing is to make an outline of your main points beforehand.

By always remembering your purpose in writing, you'll keep yourself from wandering off track. You'll also avoid confusing the reader. If you don't understand what you're trying to say, how can you expect the reader to?

2. Know your audience.

Effective writing of all kinds is tailored to its audience. Who—and how many people—will be reading the document? How familiar are they with the subject matter? Make sure the answers to these questions fit with the tone and level of detail you include in your document.

Another key is knowing how long your reader or readers will have to read your memo, report, or email. This will help to determine its length. One frequently used guideline is one double-spaced page per minute.

3. Present the most important points first.
A legal report is not a murder mystery; your reader shouldn't have to guess what the conclusion will be. Present the most important point(s) at the beginning of your document; then use the paragraphs and sections that follow to support your conclusion.

The same goes for paragraphs and sections within the document. At the beginning of each new paragraph or section, state the main point. Then present the explanation or supporting details, preferably in descending order of importance. This theory works for individual sentences, too: Placing the most important words at the beginning and end of a sentence heightens their emphasis.

4. Be concise.
The first key to being concise is using short sentences and paragraphs. Avoid sentences that are longer than 20 to 25 words long (15 words is even better!). Or simply break up

sentences that extend more than two lines. In general, no paragraph should include more than one or two ideas, and a paragraph of more than six sentences is almost always too long. When in doubt, split paragraphs in two.

The second key to being concise is eliminating unnecessary words. Qualifiers such as "very," "fairly," and "quite" rarely add meaning. In fact, because they're so overused, they often have the opposite effect. Many commonly used phrases include useless words. Replace "the question as to whether" with "whether"; "in spite of the fact that" with "although"; and "in the event that" with "if." Other wordy phrases and their replacements are listed below:

Replace:	With:
a majority of	most
at this point in time	now
due to the fact that	because
in all probability	probably
in connection with	about
in order that, in order to	to

in reference to, in regard to	about
pursuant to	since
regarding the matter of	about
utilize	use

The more concise your writing is, the clearer it will be.

5. Use simple, concrete language.

Some people think using complex language makes them appear intelligent; in reality, it only obscures their point and makes them look pretentious. Effective writers use simple words such as "start" instead of "commence," "help" instead of "assist," and "end" rather than "terminate." They also avoid technical terms and jargon, no matter how savvy the audience.

Good writers also choose concrete words and specific examples over abstract, vague language. "A watch that allows you to send email" is a much clearer description than "an IP-enabled wristwatch." One trick is to write like you talk. If something doesn't sound right when you read it out loud, change it.

6. Use the active rather than passive voice.

"I used the active voice in writing this book," sounds better than, "The active voice was used by me in writing this book," doesn't it?

7. Provide guideposts for your reader.

Help your reader by providing signals and guideposts. Transitional words and phrases (such as "and," "furthermore," "even so," and "therefore") work to connect your thoughts and indicate what's to come. Another way to create transitions is to repeat a word or a phrase from the preceding paragraph.

ALSO AVAILABLE FROM ASPATORE

EXECENABLERS ™ — GET UP TO SPEED FAST!

ExecEnablers help you determine what to read so that you can get up to speed on a new topic fast, with the right books, magazines, web sites, and other publications (from over 30,000 business publishing sources). The 2-step process involves an approximately 30 minute phone call and then a report written by Aspatore Business Editors and mailed (or emailed) to you the following day (rush/same day options available-please call 1-866-Aspatore). Only $49 Perfect for new projects, reports, classes…

Best Selling Books

MANAGEMENT/CONSULTING

Empower Profits –The Secrets to Cutting Costs & Making Money in ANY Economy
Building an Empire-The 10 Most Important Concepts to Focus a Business on the Way to Dominating the Business World
Leading CEOs-CEOs Reveal the Secrets to Leadership & Profiting in Any Economy
Leading Consultants - Industry Leaders Share Their Knowledge on the Art of Consulting
Recession Profiteers- How to Profit in a Recession & Wipe Out the Competition
Managing & Profiting in a Down Economy – Leading CEOs Reveal the Secrets to Increased Profits and Success in a Turbulent Economy
Leading Women-What It Takes to Succeed & Have It All in the 21st Century
Management & Leadership-How to Get There, Stay There, and Empower Others
Human Resources & Building a Winning Team-Retaining Employees & Leadership
Become a CEO-The Golden Rules to Rising the Ranks of Leadership
Leading Deal Makers-Leveraging Your Position and the Art of Deal Making
The Art of Deal Making-The Secrets to the Deal Making Process
Management Consulting Brainstormers – Question Blocks & Idea Worksheets

TECHNOLOGY

Leading CTOs-Leading CTOs Reveal the Secrets to the Art, Science & Future of Technology
Software Product Management-Managing Software Development from Idea to Development to Marketing to Sales
The Wireless Industry-Leading CEOs Share Their Knowledge on The Future of the Wireless Revolution
Know What the CTO Knows - The Tricks of the Trade and Ways for Anyone to Understand the Language of the Techies
Web 2.0 – The Future of the Internet and Technology Economy
The Semiconductor Industry-Leading CEOs Share Their Knowledge on the Future of Semiconductors
Techie Talk- The Tricks of the Trade and Ways to Develop, Implement and Capitalize on the Best Technologies in the World
Technology Brainstormers – Question Blocks & Idea Development Worksheets

VENTURE CAPITAL/ENTREPRENEURIAL

Term Sheets & Valuations-A Detailed Look at the Intricacies of Term Sheets & Valuations
Deal Terms- The Finer Points of Deal Structures, Valuations, Term Sheets, Stock Options and Getting Deals Done
Leading Deal Makers-Leveraging Your Position and the Art of Deal Making
The Art of Deal Making-The Secrets to the Deal Making Process
Hunting Venture Capital-Understanding the VC Process and Capturing an Investment
The Golden Rules of Venture Capitalists –Valuing Companies, Identifying Opportunities, Detecting Trends, Term Sheets and Valuations
Entrepreneurial Momentum- Gaining Traction for Businesses of All Sizes to Take the Step to the Next Level
The Entrepreneurial Problem Solver- Entrepreneurial Strategies for Identifying Opportunities in the Marketplace
Entrepreneurial Brainstormers – Question Blocks & Idea Development Worksheets

LEGAL

Privacy Matters – Leading Privacy Visionaries Share Their Knowledge on How Privacy on the Internet Will Affect Everyone

Leading Lawyers – Legal Visionaries Share Their Knowledge on the Future Legal Issues That Will Shape Our World

Leading Labor Lawyers-Labor Chairs Reveal the Secrets to the Art & Science of Labor Law

Leading Litigators-Litigation Chairs Revel the Secrets to the Art & Science of Litigation

Leading IP Lawyers-IP Chairs Reveal the Secrets to the Art & Science of IP Law

Leading Patent Lawyers –The & Science of Patent Law

Internet Lawyers-Important Answers to Issues For Every Entrepreneur, Lawyer & Anyone With a Web Site

Legal Brainstormers – Question Blocks & Idea Development Worksheets

FINANCIAL

Textbook Finance - The Fundamentals We Should All Know (And Remember) About Finance

Know What the CFO Knows - Leading CFOs Reveal What the Rest of Us Should Know About the Financial Side of Companies

Leading Accountants-The Golden Rules of Accounting & the Future of the Accounting Industry and Profession

Leading Investment Bankers-Leading I-Bankers Reveal the Secrets to the Art & Science of Investment Banking

The Financial Services Industry-The Future of the Financial Services Industry & Professions

MARKETING/ADVERTISING/PR

Leading Marketers-Leading Chief Marketing Officers Reveal the Secrets to Building a Billion Dollar Brand

Emphatic Marketing-Getting the World to Notice and Use Your Company

Leading Advertisers-Advertising CEOs Reveal the Tricks of the Advertising Profession

The Art of PR-Leading PR CEOs Reveal the Secrets to the Public Relations Profession

The Art of Building a Brand –The Secrets to Building Brands

The Golden Rules of Marketing – Leading Marketers Reveal the Secrets to Marketing, Advertising and Building Successful Brands

PR Visionaries-The Golden Rules of PR

Textbook Marketing - The Fundamentals We Should All Know (And Remember) About Marketing

Know What the VP of Marketing Knows –What Everyone Should Know About Marketing, For the Rest of Us Not in Marketing

Marketing Brainstormers – Question Blocks & Idea Development Worksheets

Guerrilla Marketing-The Best of Guerrilla Marketing-Big Marketing Ideas For a Small Budget

The Art of Sales - The Secrets for Anyone to Become a Rainmaker and Why Everyone in a Company Should be a Salesperson

The Art of Customer Service –The Secrets to Lifetime Customers, Clients and Employees Through Impeccable Customer Service

GENERAL INTEREST

ExecRecs- Executive Recommendations For The Best Products, Services & Intelligence Executives Use to Excel

The Business Translator-Business Words, Phrases & Customs in Over 90 Languages

Well Read-The Reference for Must Read Business Books & More...

Business Travel Bible (BTB) -- Must Have Information for Business Travelers

Business Grammar, Style & Usage-Rules for Articulate and Polished Business Writing and Speaking

To Order or For Customized Suggestions From an Aspatore Business Editor, Please Call 1-866-Aspatore (277-2867) Or Visit www.Aspatore.com

ASPATORE
C-Level Business Intelligence™